THE WILL OF GOD

THE WILL OF GOD

Understanding and Pursuing His Ultimate Plan for Your Life

Charles F. Stanley

HOWARD BOOKS

ATRIA

New York   London   Toronto   Sydney   New Delhi

An Imprint of Simon & Schuster, Inc.
1230 Avenue of the Americas
New York, NY 10020

First Howard Books/Atria Paperback edition October 2020

HOWARD BOOKS / ATRIA PAPERBACK and colophon are trademarks of Simon & Schuster, Inc.

For information about special discounts for bulk purchases, please contact Simon & Schuster Special Sales at 1-866-506-1949 or business@simonandschuster.com.

The Simon & Schuster Speakers Bureau can bring authors to your live event. For more information or to book an event, contact the Simon & Schuster Speakers Bureau at 1-866-248-3049 or visit our website at www.simonspeakers.com.

Interior design by Davina Mock-Maniscalco

Manufactured in the United States of America

3   4   5   7   10   8   6   4   2

Library of Congress Cataloging-in-Publication Data
Names: Stanley, Charles F., author.
Title: The will of God : understanding and pursuing his ultimate plan for your life / by Charles F. Stanley.
Description: New York : Howard Books, [2019]
Identifiers: LCCN 2019000893 (print) | LCCN 2019005063 (ebook) | ISBN 9781982104818 (eBook) | ISBN 9781982104795 (hardcover) | ISBN 9781982104818 (ebk.)
Subjects: LCSH: God (Christianity)—Will. | Discernment (Christian theology)
Classification: LCC BT135 (ebook) | LCC BT135 .S785 2019 (print) | DDC 248.4—dc23. LC record available at https://lccn.loc.gov/2019000893

ISBN 978-1-9821-0479-5
ISBN 978-1-9821-0480-1 (pbk.)
ISBN 978-1-9821-0481-8 (ebook)

CONTENTS

THE WILL OF GOD

STEP IN

A Starting Place on the Journey

The will of God.

We talk about it in church and our Christian circles enough. We hear repeatedly that the Lord has a plan for us and that it is good. We are instructed to seek it, embrace it, and live it. We are even told that it is the key to our future. But what is it? Even though God's will sounds like something we would like—and even *need*—to know, the whole idea of it often stirs up more questions than answers.

After all, it is the *will*—the volition that drives the workings of the universe, the paths of empires, and the lives of all peoples—of *God*, of the all-knowing, all-powerful, unseen, indescribable Creator of all things. Who wouldn't want to be aware of such lofty information?

Yet even those of us who have been believers a long time sometimes have mistaken ideas about what the will of God really is. Some think it is special knowledge or divine and mystical revelations that the Father gives to super-spiritual people, which is not true. Still others would admit that they shy away from God's will because they believe the Lord will ask them to do what they really don't want to do. They believe God's will is always difficult, sacrificial, or heartbreaking. That's not accurate, either.

Sadly, whatever your view of it, God's will can seem grand and unreachable, can't it? In fact, after my many years in ministry, I have heard enough people talk about how frustrated they are about their Christian life that I am fully persuaded there's one ultimate reason: They do not understand the nature of the will of God, nor do they know how to find it. And if you don't understand those two things, you may feel insecure and directionless in your walk with Jesus. Both the small, daily pressures as well as the life-changing and overwhelming issues in life can make you feel as if you are under constant assault, lost, and helpless.

Maybe that's what stirred your interest in this book. Certainly, it could be that you want to honor your Savior and stay on track with what He envisions for your life. After all, He created you and knows what He intended you to be. If He has a plan for your life, who wouldn't want to experience His very best?

But that's not usually what drives people to seek God's will. Often there are questions about the future, decisions that must be made, or challenges that arise that have no foreseeable solution that drive us to our knees before the Father. Our only hope is the Lord's insight, intervention, and provision.

In other words, perhaps you're interested in the topic of God's will because you are at a crossroad and have no idea which way to turn. Or maybe you're between a rock and a hard place and see no hope of escape.

It also could be because you don't know why the Lord has waited so long to give you the desires of your heart. Is this longing part of His plan for you or isn't it?

Or maybe you simply don't understand why certain hardships have befallen you.

The problem is, of course, how do you seek out God's will? And how do you know for certain if you have heard Him correctly? There is an incredible level of frustration when you are desperate for the Lord's guidance, but heaven seems silent. We can get so discouraged that we are tempted to say, "I really don't know how to find God's will, so what I'm going to do is the best I can and hope it all works out."

But understand, you merely "wishing that everything will be all right" is not the Father's intention. It's not His best. It's not the relationship He desires to have with you. He has a very specific plan for your life—one that can and should inspire your complete confidence. He promises in Jeremiah 29:11: "I know the plans that I have for you . . . plans for welfare and not for calamity to give you a future and a hope." This is the hope each and every one of us can cling to. God has plans for you and He knows how to accomplish them in the best, most effective way possible for your particular personality, giftedness, and future.

> *God has a very specific plan for your life—one that can and should inspire your complete confidence.*

The Lord Is a Planner

So right now, set your mind on this truth: *Our God is a planner.* He is not a reactor. He did not set this world in motion to be ruled by chance or wild, unchecked forces. Nor did He create you to live without hope and purpose.

In fact, from before the beginning the Lord has been making plans for you and for me. Just think about how He created this world with a variety of landscapes, colors, animals, plants, foods, smells, and textures. He thought of everything we would ever need and innumerable objects and creatures to satisfy our needs, stir our imaginations, fascinate our minds, and give joy to our souls.

Likewise, Ephesians 1:4 tells us God "chose us in Him"—in Christ—"before the foundation of the world, that we would be holy and blameless before Him." In other words, the Father knew you and I would have the problem of being separated from Him by our sin. He understood the pain and frustration you and I would feel at not being able to reach Him, interact with Him, and receive His love because of our fallen human state. Therefore, the Lord has been strategically unfolding His grand design to send a Savior Who would forgive our sin and restore our relationship with the One for Whom our souls most yearn. And He was careful about it—God went to great lengths to show us *Who* would make us right with Him. Through the prophets, the Father began unveiling what He would do and He precisely pointed to Who our Savior would be—each prophecy and revelation narrowing down the possibility of Who could fulfill His requirements.

For example, Isaiah foretold: "A virgin will be with child and bear a son, and she will call His name Immanuel" (Isa. 7:14). This may seem like an odd prerequisite for a Savior. However, Romans 5:12 tells us: "Through one man sin entered into the world, and death through sin, and so death spread to all men, because all sinned." At the Fall, all humanity received the sin nature—every one of us is a sinner (Rom. 3:23). This is because the seed of the sin nature passes through our fathers. But this is also why the virgin birth was necessary—without a human father, our Deliverer would not receive the sin nature.

One would think this would be sufficient to distinguish Who the Savior would be. But the Lord knew that other religions would arise that would falsely declare that they were the way to Him—and they would claim virgin births as well: Buddha, Krishna, the Egyptian deities Horus and Osiris, the Persian Mithra, the Aztec Quetzalcoatl, the Chinese Lao-Tsze, and others. So, in order to protect us from their false assertions, God narrowed the identification process further. The Anointed Savior, or *Messiah*, would be a fulfillment of the covenant to Abraham and come from his line (Gen. 12:3). And not only Abraham—but a specific great-grandchild of Abraham named Judah.

Abraham fathered Isaac; Isaac's wife, Rebekah, gave birth to twins, Jacob and Esau; and Jacob had twelve sons—including a child named Judah. About Judah, Jacob prophesied, "The scepter shall not depart from Judah, nor the ruler's staff from between his feet, until Shiloh comes, and to him shall be the obedience of the peoples" (Gen. 49:10). The *scepter* was a symbol of kingship and authority, so Jacob was communicating that someone from the line of Judah would always be the ruler of Israel. Also, the word *Shiloh* means "that which belongs to him." So Jewish scholars have taken Jacob's use of the word to refer to the Messiah—that ultimately, Christ would come through Judah's line.

Eventually, a monarch was born through Judah—a man named David. Of course, David is one of Israel's most famous kings. But God restricted the possibilities of Who Christ would be even further when He told David, "Your house and your kingdom shall endure before Me forever; your throne shall be established forever" (2 Sam. 7:16)—indicating that the Redeemer would be his descendant. So the Messiah came to be known as the "Son of David" (Matt. 1:1).

One after another, the Lord God provided incredible details about Who our Savior would be, where the Messiah would be born (Mic. 5:2), when He would appear (Dan. 9:25–26), what He would do (Isa. 61), and even His main region of ministry (Isa. 9:1; Matt. 4:12–17). Thousands of these prophecies revealed the only One Who could make us right with

God—and that is Jesus. And there would be only one sacrifice that He could make to fulfill the Lord's requirements, which was His death on the cross (Isa. 53).

Step into the Plan

Why am I telling you all of this—especially at the beginning of a book on God's will? Because if you will think about how precisely the Father has planned your redemption, your home in heaven, and your rewards—you have to realize how deeply He treasures you and how carefully He thinks about your future. He wouldn't have gone to such lengths to provide for your salvation if He did not value you.

> *God made such an extraordinary and costly investment in you because He sees you're worth it. And He wants you to join Him in His great plan.*

Now think about this: Would God—having been so specific in all of His planning—suddenly just forget about you? Would He say, "Live your life the best you can. Just do what you can with what you've got"? Of course He wouldn't. He made such an extraordinary and costly investment in you because He sees you're worth it. And He wants you to join Him in His great plan.

In fact, what we see consistently throughout history is that the Father *wants* to reveal His will. He also shows us the way *into* His plan for each of us—and that is through a relationship with Jesus. In every way, Jesus is the key that opens the door to understanding God's plan and it all begins by accepting Him as your Savior.

If you have never received Jesus Christ as your Lord and Savior, it is no wonder that the whole concept of God's will is confusing to you. Many people think they can know the Lord's path for them without ever really knowing Jesus—the One Who is His ultimate plan. Don't make that mistake. The Father's purpose for your life doesn't have to remain a mystery.

So if no one has ever had the great and joyful privilege of helping you to receive Christ's gift of salvation, I pray you will allow me to do so now. All it takes is being willing to admit that you cannot overcome your sin on your own, but that you trust that the sacrifice Jesus made on the cross was sufficient to forgive everything you have ever done wrong. Are you willing? If so, you can tell Him in your own words or use this simple prayer:

Lord Jesus, I come to You asking You to forgive my sins and save me from eternal separation from God. In faith, I accept Your work and death on the cross as sufficient payment for my transgressions. I also confess that You are Lord. Help me to turn from my sins and live in a manner that is pleasing to You.

I praise You for providing the way for me to know You and to have a relationship with my heavenly Father. Through faith in You, I have eternal life and I trust You have prepared a home in heaven for me. I acknowledge that trusting You as my Savior is my first step into understanding and living out God's will.

Thank You for hearing my prayers, loving me unconditionally, and leading me in God's plan. Please give me the strength, wisdom, and determination to walk in the center of Your will. In Jesus' name, amen.

Beginning, End, and Everything in Between

If you've just received Jesus as your Lord and Savior, you've just made the very best decision you will ever make! There is absolutely nothing more important in this life or the next than having a personal relationship with God.

But whether you've just accepted Christ or have walked with Him for decades, understand that what I said to you is central and essential: Jesus is the ultimate key to knowing and living God's will. Jesus provides you with access to the throne of grace, so you can learn His plan for you (Heb. 4:16). He is

Jesus is the ultimate key to knowing and living God's will.

your example of the life of faith in every way (Rom. 8:29). His Holy Spirit guides and empowers you (John 16:13-14; 1 Cor. 2:9–16; Phil. 2:3). His prayers sustain you (Heb. 7:25). His Word provides a light to your path (Ps. 119:105).

I say this because many people believe that God's will is about living by a specific religious or moral standard or making certain decisions. And at a very basic level, it is. But it is really much more than that. It is about a profound, intimate relationship with God Himself—a relationship that results in a life that overflows with His wisdom, purpose, and power.

Ephesians 2:10 asserts: "We are His workmanship, created *in Christ Jesus* for good works, which God prepared beforehand so that we would *walk in them*" (emphasis added). Yes, the Father has created you with a reason in mind, to fulfill an important role in His kingdom. And it is *in* Jesus, as a person who is saved by Him, and *through* Jesus, as His disciple who is in fellowship with Him, that you discover, understand, and walk in His purposes.

Jesus Himself said it: "I am the way, and the truth, and the life; no one comes to the Father but through Me" (John 14:6). We often think of this verse in terms of salvation, but it is true of the Christian life as well. Jesus wants to be *your* way, *your* truth, and *your* life. In Him and through Him are the Father's will for you.

So don't mistakenly think, *God's not really interested in teaching me, leading me, or revealing His will.* Yes, He certainly is—more than you can ever imagine (Rom. 8:32). Not only is God attentive to the great and impactful circumstances of your life, but He is also observant of details so small they escape your notice. God cares about the problems, burdens, and conflicts that concern you. And what He wants most is a personal relationship with you where you walk with Him in such close union that you are consistently aware of His presence with you. Yes, He wants that. In fact, that's why He has given His own Spirit to live within you and direct you.

No, the journey of seeking and living out God's will may not be easy; in fact, I can testify it is sometimes very difficult. But it is always worthwhile. Because when you listen to and follow Him, you know what happens? You get His best. You will experience the greatest joy and fulfillment—to the deepest depths of your soul—because you will be living out the very reason you were created.

Are you willing? Then let's get started.

2

THE BIG PICTURE

Understanding What God's Goal Is

When we pick up a book on God's will, it is generally because we want to know how to discover it for a specific issue that confronts us. We are looking for the five easy steps to knowing the Lord's plan for our lives. And perhaps you are tempted to skip to the chapter with those steps rather than read through these first chapters that describe what God desires to accomplish in your life.

In fact, it is possible you read through chapter 1 thinking, *I run a business. I just need to find out how to direct my company in a godly way and there are choices ahead that are confusing to me. Jesus is already my Savior. That's not the problem.*

Or maybe you would tell me, "I'm a parent. I want to raise my children in a manner that honors God. How do I know when to hold on to them and when to let go?"

You could be a student who is simply trying to figure out which university or course of study would suit you best. Or perhaps you're a single person trying to decide whether or not you should marry the person you are dating.

You know that God is a planner and that Jesus wants to be part of your decision-making process. You desire to make wise choices. But how does what I am saying really apply to you and your situation?

Friend, what I have to tell you has absolutely everything to do with what you need. Your concerns are exactly what I am talking about.

Do Not Fear

What is important for you to understand is that the choices before you today are a part of God's bigger picture for you. They may feel like they consume your life at the moment or represent the precarious crossroad on which the success or failure of your future hinges. You may feel as if the wrong decision could ruin everything for you and those you love.

> *The choices before you today are a part of God's bigger picture for you.*

I have had many such instances in my own life. Many. And they have comprised every area of my being—from where to pastor to how to respond to failed relationships, what to do about financial and health challenges, and all the rest. I may not have experienced your exact problem, but I know how deeply the anxieties and struggles of life can overwhelm and confuse even the steadiest heart. And I know how it feels when it seems like you cannot hear God's voice.

I recall a very difficult season of seeking the Father's will during my senior year at the University of Richmond. Absolutely everything seemed to be going wrong, and I was completely miserable. It was exam week, and I had received a 50 on one test and a 75 on another. I was a senior and it seemed as if I'd spent all this time in school just to fail. I was desperate to know God's plan and purpose for my life, but it felt as if He had completely walked out on me—like He was a thousand miles away, gone and without thought for how profoundly I was hurting. Nothing I did seemed to help.

I recall praying, "Father, I've got to be absolutely sure what Your will is for me. I've prayed, asked, pleaded, begged, and fasted. I've done everything I know to do. God, please do *something*—my whole future is based on You. Please clarify this question in my mind and show me exactly what to do." Perhaps you've expressed the same kind of prayer and can relate to the pressure I was under.

But then the Lord brought to mind something my grandfather George Washington Stanley told me. He had gone through a similar time in his life, when, like me, he was confused and seeking God's guidance about whether or not to preach. So Granddad got down on his knees and asked the Father to show him what to do. Then he said, "Lord, if You are calling me to preach the gospel, let me see two falling stars." Sure enough, he looked up and saw two bright lights shoot across the night sky.

I thought to myself, *If Granddad asked God for something that specific and the Lord answered, then maybe He will do the same for me.* After all, my grandfather never doubted that the Father had called him to preach. So I prayed, "God, I know I don't have any business asking You this, but if this is Your will for my life—if this is really what You're calling me to do—please let me see two falling stars like my grandfather did." A couple of evenings later, I looked up and saw two brilliant stars streaming across the night sky at the same time.

It wasn't until I got back to my room in the dorm and I was brushing my teeth that God spoke to my heart, *What did you ask Me for?*

I replied, "Well, Lord, I've seen a falling star before."

Two at the same time?

"No."

That's right, you haven't. You've never seen that before because you've never requested it until now. You asked Me and I've answered your prayer.

Now, I will be transparent with you. I was not convinced. I had read the Word and received no answer. I had prayed and heard only silence. And so my heart was tired, full of sorrow, and resistant. Maybe you know what I mean. You become so weighed down by your own hurts and insecurities that you doubt God will ever really answer you.

I sat on my bed and thought, *Just forget it. I'm done.* But I could not shake the conviction; I was so impressed to pray one more time. And I am so grateful that I did not resist. I kneeled next to my bed and God beautifully and quietly answered what I had been asking—giving me an overwhelming sense of peace and tranquility. Immediately, I fell on my face and thanked the Lord with all my heart. If the Father had not spoken to me in such a powerful way at that point, I may have given up and my life would have been altered completely.

I tell you this story because, as I said, I understand what it feels like to beseech God for guidance and not hear Him. And what I can testify today without a shadow of a doubt is that the Lord Who created you is more than able to teach you what to do and keep you on the path of His will when you seek Him.

Do not fear!

So the first principle for you is: ***Do not fear!***

Fear can blind you to God's purposes and the very guidance you are seeking. Anxiety can cause you to lose heart, make bad decisions, and even give up completely. This is why Scripture often repeats the command:

+ "Be strong and courageous, do not be afraid or tremble at them, for the LORD your God is the one who goes with you. He will not fail you or forsake you.... The LORD is the one who goes ahead of you; He will be with you. He will not fail you or forsake you. Do not fear or be dismayed" (Deut. 31: 6, 8).

✦ "Have I not commanded you? Be strong and courageous! Do not tremble or be dismayed, for the LORD your God is with you wherever you go" (Josh. 1:9).

✦ Thus says the LORD to you, "Do not fear or be dismayed because of this great multitude, for the battle is not yours but God's" (2 Chron. 20:15).

✦ "Do not fear, for I am with you; do not anxiously look about you, for I am your God. I will strengthen you, surely I will help you, surely I will uphold you with My righteous right hand" (Isa. 41:10).

✦ Thus says the LORD, your Creator, O Jacob, and He who formed you, O Israel, "Do not fear, for I have redeemed you; I have called you by name; you are Mine! When you pass through the waters, I will be with you; and through the rivers, they will not overflow you. When you walk through the fire, you will not be scorched, nor will the flame burn you" (Isa. 43:1–2).

✦ "Do not fear, O land, rejoice and be glad, for the LORD has done great things (Joel 2:21).

✦ "Be of good cheer! It is I; do not be afraid" (Matt. 14:27).

✦ "Do not be afraid; only believe" (Mark 5:26).

+ "Do not be afraid, for behold, I bring you good tidings of great joy which will be to all people" (Luke 2:10).

+ "Peace I leave with you; My peace I give to you; not as the world gives do I give to you. Do not let your heart be troubled, nor let it be fearful" (John 14:27).

+ "Do not be afraid, but speak, and do not keep silent; for I am with you" (Acts 18:9–10).

+ "Even if you should suffer for the sake of righteousness, you are blessed. And do not fear their intimidation, and do not be troubled, but sanctify Christ as Lord in your hearts, always being ready to make a defense to everyone who asks you to give an account for the hope that is in you" (1 Pet. 3:14–15).

+ "He laid His right hand on me, saying to me, 'Do not be afraid; I am the First and the Last. I am He who lives, and was dead, and behold, I am alive forevermore'" (Rev. 1:17–18).

Therefore, set your heart to reject fear. Do not be afraid that you are unworthy of knowing His will. He makes you worthy (Rom. 8:31–34). Do not fear that you are somehow disqualified from His love, plan, and protection. No one can take you out of His hand once you've accepted Christ as your Savior—not even you (John 10:28–29). Do not fear that you won't or can't hear God. He created you and can break through to you.

Breaking Through

The ability to hear God is one of the greatest mysteries and areas of frustration for many believers. How can someone truly know he or she has a promise or answer from the Lord—especially as the days pass without confirmation or circumstances go awry? As I told you in the previous section, I have wrestled with this issue myself. He is God and we are not. Even in our interactions with other people, whom we can see with our eyes and hear with our physical ears, we often mistake their meaning. And the Lord is spiritual—we cannot see Him, touch Him, or sit face to face with Him. How can we ever be certain that we are hearing Him and not our own hearts?

However, Hebrews 1:1–2 teaches us: "God, after He spoke long ago to the fathers in the prophets in many portions and in many ways, in these last days has spoken to us in His Son." In other words, the Lord is actively speaking to us and wants to communicate with us. He tells us, "Call to Me and I will answer you, and I will tell you great and mighty things, which you do not know" (Jer. 33:3). The Father bids us to approach Him and He promises to get through to us with information that does not originate with us.

Understanding and believing that God speaks is one of the biggest differences between a person experiencing the extraordinary, fruitful Christian life and the one just practicing religion. Therefore, if you wish to know and walk in the Father's will for you, this is the second principle you must

Believe that God speaks in a manner you can hear.

set your heart on: **You must believe that God speaks in a manner you can hear.**

God is not like the person whom you write to, call, and reach out to repeatedly, but who never answers you back. He is not the delivery service that loses your letter or package. He is not the family member who refuses to interact with you. He says, "You will seek Me and find *Me*, when you search for Me with all your heart" (Jer. 29:13). Likewise, Jesus—God Himself—promised, "Ask, and it will be given to you; seek, and you will find; knock, and it will be opened to you" (Matt. 7:7). This does not mean the Lord will answer you immediately, but He will indeed respond to your cries.

Of course, the fact that God speaks may not be the issue for you. Perhaps your fear is that even though you're seeking Him, you cannot hear Him. But remember, Hebrews 1:1 says, "God, after He spoke long ago to the fathers in the prophets *in many portions and in many ways*" (emphasis added). He spoke to people at different times, with various methods, and in diverse manners. Even the amount He disclosed to His people was specific and measured. Isn't that interesting? There is not one way the Lord speaks—but many, according to whom He is speaking to and what He is revealing.

Think about it: How did God communicate with Adam and Eve? He walked with them in the cool of the day as a Father who teaches His children (Gen. 3:8). How did the Lord talk to Moses? He did so from a burning bush—a phenomenon that not only caught Moses' attention but also showed him God could do the miraculous (Exod. 3). Likewise, the Father spoke to Joseph through dreams (Gen. 37:5–9), to Elijah in the "sound of a gentle blowing" (1 Kings 19:12), to Joshua through the mighty "captain of the host of the LORD" (Josh. 5:14), to Saul through the prophet

God is not limited with how He communicates His plan.

Samuel (1 Sam. 9:27), to Jonah through a large fish (Jonah 1:17), to the people of God through the reading of His Word (Neh. 8), and to John through the heavenly vision (Rev. 1). Are you getting the picture? God is not limited with how He communicates His plan.

But why? Why did the Lord see fit to use so many methods? Could it be that the God Who knit us together in our mothers' wombs knows the best way to get our attention and declare His will to us? Absolutely. Friend, the Father knows what we can handle, what we are prepared to hear, and the best way to reveal it to us.

So really, it is crucial for you to see that the God Who created this earth can surmount any inability you have to hear Him. Not only is it imperative that you believe the Father that communicates with you, but you also must believe God speaks *in a manner you can hear.*

However, here is a caveat to this principle that is crucial that we comprehend: The Father reserves the right to accept your *refusal* to hear Him. What do I mean by this? Well, often we think, *I've been listening and can't hear a thing from the Lord.* We believe in our hearts that we want *His will,* but we what we really want is for Him to do things our way. So we are resistant to what He is saying and never fully convinced we've heard Him or that He is speaking. There are generally three ways this can happen:

✦ *God has spoken and you don't like His answer, so you refuse to accept it.* An example of this is the prophet Jonah, who was tasked with preaching to the cruel enemies of Israel in Nineveh. Because of his prejudice against the Ninevites, Jonah ran from the assignment.

Likewise, there are times God will call us to do difficult things such as forgive someone who has hurt us deeply, sacrifice something we care about, or take on a burden that we believe will limit our freedom. We cannot see how this is key to His will being accomplished in our lives. But realize that God does not require us to understand His will, just obey it, even if it seems unreasonable. The Father would not ask it of you unless He saw something important in your life that requires it—something you may be blind to.

> *Whenever you get stuck hearing from the Father, always go back to the last thing God told you and do it—even if it does not make sense to you.*

So whenever you get stuck hearing from the Father, always go back to the last thing God told you and do it—even if it does not make sense to you.

✦ ***The Lord has spoken and you can't believe His answer, so you think you heard Him wrong.*** This is what I can call a faith issue. Our inadequacies, adverse circumstances, and the lies that are planted deep within our hearts convince us that God won't really come through for us. We simply cannot see how He will accomplish all He said He would.

For example, after the people of Israel left Egypt, they traveled to the land God had promised them, knowing that they would face opposition. However, when they got there, they discovered "the people living there are powerful, and their towns are large and fortified. We even saw giants there" (Num. 13:28 NLT). These appeared to be impossible obstacles. The Israelites were so frightened by the prospect of having to go in and conquer the land that they gave up without even trying. They simply could not see how God would deliver the Promised Land over to them.

However, this is why Proverbs 3:5–6 admonishes: "Trust in the LORD with all your heart and do not lean on your own understanding. In all your ways acknowledge Him, and He will make your paths straight." You don't have to know how God will accomplish it, just that He has never gone back on His promises to anyone (Josh. 21:45; 1 Kings 8:56). Trust what He tells you.

✦ *The Father has not yet spoken because you don't need to know yet.* In other words, the Lord is willing to speak to you, but you have put artificial time limits on when He should. This is perhaps the most frustrating reason for people who are seeking God's will. We believe we have both a need and a right to know information as soon as we ask for it. But often we need to wait because of purposes unseen to us.

For example, several years ago I was in an accident that wrecked my automobile. As I was riding in the ambulance to the hospital, the Lord spoke to me very clearly: "Do not buy another car." I thought this was odd, but the Father's command was so strong that I felt I couldn't ignore it. So I obeyed Him and someone graciously lent me a vehicle to drive. The loaner I was given was a sight to behold. It was one of those old, beat-up, gas-guzzling Cadillacs—enormous, long, and clunky, with checkered seats, fins, and its own zip code. I was grateful for the loan, but I confess I was incredibly embarrassed about being seen in it. I would hold my hand up to my face at stoplights so people wouldn't recognize me.

In the days that followed, people kept asking me, "Charles, when are you going to get a car?" I just kept telling them that I was waiting for God to show me what to do. I lived this way for more than a year. Finally, the wait and the ridicule got to be too much for me. I gave in to my desire to buy an automobile and went down to a local dealership. There was a car there that I thought would be acceptable. But I test-drove it three times and never felt quite right about it. Each time, the Lord spoke to me in a manner I will never forget: "Do you want this or do you want My best?" There was no question in my mind about that, so I replied, "Father, I want Your best. I'm going to trust You."

It was a week or two later that I rode with a church member to an important meeting. I didn't know him all that well, but he offered to pick me up and take me. So I went, glad to have the opportunity to spend some time with him.

Along the way he asked, "Charles, when are you going to get yourself a car?" I thought to myself, *Oh goodness, not this again.* But I managed to answer, "Well, I don't know. God just hasn't given me permission to buy one yet for some reason."

"What would you choose if you could get anything you wanted?" he inquired.

The words were out of my mouth before I could think about it: "One just like this," I replied. This man had a very fine vehicle, one far better than I had ever considered purchasing for myself. Three days later, I received a check to buy an automobile just like his—a car far superior than I had hoped for or could have imagined. And it was absolutely free.

God didn't tell me what to do about that automobile because He was working in the unseen to orchestrate a blessing for me. The same is true for you. Don't give up because the Father has not given you an answer yet. He knows the exact timing for *when* you need to hear Him.

> *Don't give up because the Father has not given you an answer yet. He knows the exact timing for when you need to hear Him.*

Of course, these are broad-stroke reasons why we don't hear God when He speaks. There are underlying causes as well, which we will look at further in a subsequent chapter. The point is, however, that the Father is indeed speaking to you and desires for you to hear Him. And the main subject of His communication with you is teaching you the central focus of His will, which is making you more like Jesus.

Not To, but For

We learn that God's goal for us is becoming like Jesus from Romans 8:29, which teaches: "Those whom He foreknew, He also predestined to become conformed to the image of His Son." Therefore, we can say without a shadow of doubt that this is what the Father wants to do in you—that His ultimate objective for you is to look like Jesus in character and conduct.

So in chapter 12 of Romans, Paul describes what this looks like. Verse 1 tells us: "I urge you, brethren, by the mercies of God, to present your bodies a living and holy sacrifice, acceptable to God, which is your spiritual service of worship."

Why did Paul feel it necessary to teach this? As he wrote this letter to the Romans, the Jewish people were still making their offerings twice a day at the temple in Jerusalem—as they had been for a long time. If anyone understood sacrifices, it was the people of Israel. We know that when Solomon built the temple and the people of Israel went to dedicate it they "were sacrificing so many sheep and oxen that they could not be counted or numbered" (2 Chron. 5:6). They were very good at making their sacrifices.

You see this throughout Israel's history. They presented *guilt offerings* for when they sinned intentionally (Lev. 5). They gave *sin offerings* when they sinned unintentionally (Lev. 6:24–30). They furnished *burnt offerings* to show that they were devoted to God and rejected sin (Lev. 6:8–13). They provided *grain offerings*—to show respect to the Lord and acknowledge all they had was from Him (Lev. 6:14–23). And they supplied *fellowship* or *peace offerings*—to express gratitude to the Father and honor their relationship with Him (Lev. 7:11–21).

In fact, the Jewish historian Josephus reported that around the time when Paul was writing Romans they counted the Passover lambs that were sacrificed in a three-hour period of time and it was more than 256,000.[1] That is more than a quarter of a million lambs that were offered in just three hours. If anyone knew how to make sacrifices, the Israelites did.

However, a relationship with God is not just about making sacrifices *to* Him. This was where the Jews made their mistake and why Paul felt the need to address it in his letter to the Romans. You see, the Lord doesn't just want things *from* you—He wants *you.*

> The Lord doesn't just want things from *you*— He wants you.

---

[1] Flavius Josephus, *The Complete Works* (Grand Rapids, MI: Christian Classics Ethereal Library), 1241.

His desire is not merely for you to *make* sacrifices, but for you to *be* surrendered for His use.

For example, perhaps you sense the Lord convicting you to give up certain bad habits and sinful behaviors such as gossiping or disparaging others. So you think, *I just won't tell others how much I hate that person or the awful things that person has done.* But is that the right attitude? Does that truly represent the heart of a person who has presented his or her body as a living and holy sacrifice, acceptable to God?

Well, Proverbs 10:18 tells us, "He who conceals hatred has lying lips." So if you despise someone and keep it to yourself, God's Word says you are a liar. However, Proverbs 10:18 also says, "He who spreads slander is a fool." So if you talk about what you detest about others, you're both a slanderer and a fool. In other words, you should not keep your complaints about others to yourself, nor should you talk about them. Why would Scripture present such a no-win scenario? I believe that this is because our temptation is to deal with our sin outwardly instead of where it is rooted.

You see, what God really wants you to do is to forgive the person you dislike and love him or her as He would (Eph. 4:32). He wants you to purge the angry feelings from your heart and forgive as He does.

Friend, it's not just your external acts that need to be put on the altar. It is not just your tithe, a particular habit, or some treasured object. Your heart—in fact, everything about you—is the sacrifice your heavenly Father requires. Remember, the Lord says, "I delight in *loyalty* rather than sacrifice, and in the knowledge of God rather than burnt offerings" (Hosea 6:6, emphasis added). The word for *loyalty* there is the Hebrew word *chesed*, and it can also be translated as *love, goodness, kindness,* and *faithfulness*. It is best expressed in love that reveals itself through a godly life and has its root in a relationship with the Father where you truly know Him. This is a word closely associated with the character of God, and that's the point—He wants us to reflect His character. He wants His spiritual fruit of love, joy, peace, patience, kindness, goodness, faithfulness, gentleness, and self-control to flow through us (Gal. 5:22–23). To Him, that is always far more important than outward sacrifices.

After all, what were all of those Old Testaments sacrifices and offerings supposed to point us to? Jesus. And whose image are we being conformed to? Jesus'. We are becoming living sacrifices as He has shown us to be. So that is our next principle: *We have to stop thinking we are making offerings to God and realize we are becoming a living sacrifice for Him.*

We have to stop thinking we are making offerings to God and realize we are becoming a living sacrifice for Him.

We are free from making offerings to prove our loyalty or devotion to the Lord or even to appease His anger. Jesus already did that on the cross for us. Rather, this is our "spiritual service of worship" (Rom. 12:1), which means we are acknowledging Who God is. He is the Lord God, the Creator of heaven and earth, the Only True and Everlasting God, our Savior, who deserves our wholehearted devotion and praise. So we transfer our rights to our lives to Him and become sacrifices for Him in this world by being His representatives, His ambassadors (2 Cor. 5:20–21). First Peter 2:9 tells us, "You are a chosen race, a royal priesthood, a holy nation, a people for God's own possession, so that you may proclaim the excellencies of Him who has called you out of darkness into His marvelous light." We are not paying God off; we're gratefully giving our lives to the One Who has given all for us.

Because, when you think about it, not only are we His by right of the fact that He created us, but all of us who are believers are also His by re-demption. Likewise, we are being conformed to the image of Christ, and isn't that what Jesus did—become a ransom for us in obedience to the Father? Jesus did not merely make offerings to God; He became the ulti-mate sacrifice in order to carry out the Lord's sacred and holy mission. And that purpose was so we could have a relationship with Him.

So this is God's will for your life—for you to look like Jesus, which be-gins by presenting yourself as a holy sacrifice unto the Lord. But for most people, this is a difficult prospect to accept. In light of this, before we go any further, I ask you to pray to God to make you receptive to what I have to teach you. You can say something like this: "Lord, please make me sensi-tive and responsive to what You want me to understand." Because this is exceedingly important if you truly desire to walk in God's will.

The Specifics: The *Basis* of Our Surrender

Once we understand the Father's main goal for us, there is more we can glean from Romans 12. First, we should note that we are called to be living sacrifices "by the mercies of God" (v. 1). In other words, we are not called to be completely His on the basis of His anger, control issues, or condem-nation. We are called to surrender everything to Him because of His mercy and compassion toward us.

Just look at your life and all the ways the Father has expressed mercy to you and those you love. He is tender toward you, forgiving, generous, and loving. We must take note of this because we cannot really worship God genuinely and wholeheartedly until we come to the place of recog-nizing how much He has blessed us and how gracious He's been to us. No one can serve the Lord with real passion until they are persuaded of the everlasting and overwhelming kindness of God. We know this was certainly true for the apostle Paul. He wrote: "It is a trustworthy statement, deserving full acceptance, that Christ Jesus came into the world to save sinners, among whom I am foremost of all" (1 Tim. 1:15). The apostle Paul saw himself as a man unworthy of the grace the Lord Jesus had shown him.

There is so much wisdom in this. Paul understood the incredible price that Jesus paid for us and what a tremendous gift our salvation truly is. He realized that he did not deserve Christ's mercy or forgiveness and was always grateful for it. This is so refreshing considering the attitudes of many today. I have met believers who felt entitled to salvation, as if they were doing Jesus a favor by believing in Him. I find this mind-set heartbreaking because they don't grasp the astounding compassion God has shown them.

Of course, it's not very popular to talk about the depth of our destitution and despair before Jesus becomes our Savior—the fact that we are spiritually dead in our transgressions (Eph. 2:1), separated from God forever (Eph. 2:12), and on track for the lake of fire (Rev. 2:15). However, it is necessary to do so in order for us to appreciate what we have been given and realize the heart with which the Father provided it. As Paul writes in Romans 8:32, "He who did not spare His own Son, but delivered Him over for us all, how will He not also with Him freely give us all things?" God understood the depth of our spiritual poverty and rescued us because of His love for us. And that is the same attitude by which Jesus says, "Whoever wishes to save his life will lose it, but whoever loses his life for My sake and the gospel's will save it" (Mark 8:35). He sees beyond what we do to what is eternal and would truly satisfy our hearts—and He desires for us to experience His abundant life.

So this is a principle we need to grasp with all our heart, soul, mind, and strength: **We are called to surrender everything to Him out of gratefulness for His mercy and compassion toward us.** We do so because He loves us and knows what is best for us even better than we do.

> *We are called to surrender everything to Him out of gratefulness for His mercy and compassion toward us.*

The Specifics: The *Manner* of Our Surrender

The next truth Paul teaches in Romans 12 is the *manner* of our surrender. How do we change from business as usual to walking in God's will and becoming the living sacrifices that exalt Him? In verse 2, Paul explains, "Do not be conformed to this world, but be transformed by the renewing of your mind, so that you may prove what the will of God is, that which is good and acceptable and perfect."

We need to examine what he is saying closely, because it is very instructive. First, he says, "Do not be conformed." The word for *conformed* is *syschematizo*, which means to adapt yourself—your mind, character, habits, bearing, discourse, actions, and manner of life—to another's pattern. It can mean being pressed into a mold or being stamped by the likeness of something. If you have ever seen a chameleon jump from the green grass to a red flower or a brown branch, you have seen this concept in action. The chameleon almost instantly changes color to blend in with its new situation—it protects itself by conforming, by avoiding standing out. And that is what we do in this world.

In fact, this word for *conformed* is used in only two places in the Bible—

here in Romans 12:2 and in 1 Peter 1:14–15, which says, "As obedient children, do not be conformed to the former lusts which were yours in your ignorance, but like the Holy One who called you, be holy yourselves also in all your behavior." It is interesting to note that Peter does not attribute our sinful acts to being enlightened to worldly ways or free to live as we please—but to our ignorance.

What Peter is referencing here is something I have spoken of often, which is what occurred at the Fall (Gen. 3). Perhaps you recall that the Father instructed Adam and Eve not to eat from a certain tree in the Garden of Eden. "The LORD God commanded the man, saying, 'From any tree of the garden you may eat freely; but from the tree of the knowledge of good and evil you shall not eat, for in the day that you eat from it you will surely die'" (Gen. 2:16–17). Of course, we know Adam and Eve eventually disobeyed and ate of the tree of the knowledge of good and evil despite God's command and warning (Gen. 3).

What ensued was that Adam and Eve received a great deal of information that they were unequipped to handle without God's guidance. Good and evil were put on equal footing in their knowledge and comprehension. Yes, there were certain actions that they knew to be immoral from the beginning—such as murder and stealing (Rom. 1:18–25). But because their sin caused them to die spiritually, they lost the capacity to discern right from wrong as they would have learned if they had allowed the Lord to teach them. This is why Scripture teaches: "There is a way which seems right to a man, but its end is the way of death" (Prov. 16:25). We don't realize that the ways we are filling our needs are actually caus-

It takes a relationship with Christ to truly understand how to have our needs met—that is, what's God's will for us.

ing us to feel emptier and more destitute. It takes a relationship with Christ to truly understand how to have those needs met—that is, what's God's will for us and what isn't.

This is why Peter says we commit sin in ignorance—we do not know any better. However, because we know Jesus as our Savior, we don't have to keep being blinded to what we are doing that undermines our well-being.

This is why after we accept Jesus as our Savior we understand that there are aspects of how we operate that must change. The Holy Spirit convicts us of beliefs and behaviors that otherwise we would accept as normal. And as we debate whether or not to make the change He is asking of us, we may look at the world with some confusion, thinking, *I thought this was natural—the reality of how people function and how we are built.* So even as Christians we will continually be tempted to remain trapped in our sins, because we think of it as how we are wired.

But what is it that Romans 12:2 tells us not to conform to? Our English translation tells us that we should avoid being pressed into the mold of "this world" (v. 2). However, the Greek is much more specific. The word there is *aion*, which can be translated as *age* or *time period*. That gives us a great deal to think about, because one of the main complaints we hear against the Bible is that it is antiquated—old-fashioned, unenlightened, and unable to keep up with the trends of our culture. I even hear this from misled pastors, who claim that Scripture does not deal adequately with the struggles people are facing in today's day and age.

But that is exactly the problem—the focus is on *this age*. What they fail to understand is that we may have a unique *expression* of the human struggle with sin today, but the underlying problem is the same as it has always been. Since the Fall, people have always wrestled with issues of identity, dominance, wealth, acceptance, worth, sexuality, and all the rest. So the way most choose to cope with their felt needs is by turning to the technologies, solutions, and accepted behaviors of *this age*, which promise to be better than ever before. What people fail to understand, however, is that like every other man-made solution, it can only fleetingly dull the cavernous pain they feel temporarily, because it does not reach down into the true source of the hurt.

As you read this, the same is true for you and the battle or decision you are facing. Understand, "there is nothing new under the sun" (Eccl. 1:9). The enemy will try to discourage you with thoughts of isolation—that the reason you are suffering it is because you are singularly unworthy of God's help and intervention or because you are not living by the ways of "this age." But nothing could be further from the truth. In fact, Peter affirmed this, saying, "Be of sober spirit, be on the alert. Your adversary, the devil, prowls around like a roaring lion, seeking someone to devour. But resist him, firm in your faith, knowing that the same experiences of suffering are being accomplished by your brethren who are in the world" (1 Pet. 5:8–9).

You are not alone. Your situation is something God has handled again and again throughout the ages. In fact, it is a tool He is using to teach you how to walk with Him. Nothing that "this age" offers will ever meet the profound questions and needs you feel. Moreover, it's the ways you are clinging to your present understanding of the world and human interactions that may be hindering you.

> *Your situation is a tool God is using to teach you how to walk with Him.*

Therefore, instead of viewing today's issues as unique and conforming ourselves to the views of this age, Romans 12:2 tells us to be "be transformed by the renewing of your mind." The word *transformed* is *metamorphoo*, which literally means to change into another form. This word is used only four times in the Bible, two of which are in reference to Jesus at the

Transfiguration. Matthew 17:2 tells us, "He was transfigured before them; and His face shone like the sun, and His garments became as white as light." Jesus' transformation was supernatural, so we know that which occurs within us must also be beyond this natural world.

Likewise, we can have confidence that this transformation will occur in us because the other time the word *metamorphoo* is used in Scripture is in 2 Corinthians 3:18, which says, "We all, with unveiled face, beholding as in a mirror the glory of the Lord, *are being transformed* into the same image from glory to glory just as from the Lord, the Spirit" (emphasis added). Therefore, this is a transformation under way in us, and of course the image Paul speaks of here is the likeness of the Lord Jesus.

But how are we actually being transformed? After all, if this metamorphosis is supernatural, then this is not something we are enacting ourselves. Romans 12:2 teaches it happens "by the renewing of our minds." So the key to transformation is changing *what* and *how* we think.

Just to clarify, however, this is not merely about having new opinions or adopting a different system of beliefs. Sometimes we assume that's what religion is—you change the name of the deity, what the sacrifice is, and some of the behaviors, but that's all there really is to it. But there is more God wants to do in us—and that is revolutionize us from the inside out.

> *God wants to revolutionize us from the inside out.*

In fact, the word Paul uses for renewing is *anakainosis*, which can be translated as *renewal, renovation,* and *a complete change for the better.* It comes from the root word *anakainoo*, which means to cause to grow up, to make new, to be changed into a new kind of life as opposed to the former corrupt state. Therefore, we know that when our minds are renewed it means we change the way we process information.

But there is more we can glean from the word *anakainosis*. The only other place it is used in Scripture is in Paul's letter to Titus, when he writes: "He saved us, not on the basis of deeds which we have done in righteousness, but according to His mercy, by the washing of regeneration and *renewing* by the Holy Spirit" (Titus 3:5, emphasis added). Here Paul is talking about salvation, but we should take note of Who accomplishes it in us. Of course, it is God's own Spirit Who does the work. He teaches us to think in a different way. We don't take the outward form of the world, but rather, inwardly we are completely transformed by the internal influence of the Holy Spirit as we read God's Word and pray. Paul explains:

> It is written, "Things which eye has not seen and ear has not heard, and which have not entered the heart of man, all that God has prepared for those who love Him." For to us God revealed them through the Spirit; for the Spirit searches all things, even the depths of God. . . . Now we have received, not the spirit of the world, but the Spirit who is from God, so that we may know the things freely given to us by God. . . . He who is spiritual appraises all things, yet he himself is appraised by no one. For who has known the mind of the Lord, that he will instruct Him? But we have the mind of Christ (1 Cor. 2:9–10, 12, 15–16).

In other words, with a natural, unredeemed mind we could never perceive the great plans God has for us or how to live in them. But we have a completely different mind—one that is much greater because we have the very thoughts of God through the presence of the Holy Spirit. We have "the mind of Christ" (v. 16). That is astounding! When we allow God to transform us by the renewing of our minds in order to become living sacrifices, we have access to His all-knowing, all-powerful, perfect mind.

Good, Acceptable, Perfect

If that does not inspire you I don't know what will. Because when we have His mind, we also know His will. In fact, that's what the last phrase of Romans 12:2 promises: "Do not be conformed to this world, but be transformed by the renewing of your mind, *so that you may prove what the will of God is, that which is good and acceptable and perfect*" (emphasis added). You will be able to scrutinize opportunities and ideas and judge whether or not they are worthy—whether or not they are from the Lord Himself. This is what it takes to be a living sacrifice, after all, to know God's will, be empowered to carry it out in His way, and actually accomplish it for His glory.

But notice that the will of God is "good and acceptable and perfect." It doesn't say that the Lord's plan for you will be unbearable, that you'll hate it, and that it will ruin your life. On the contrary, what the Father envisions for you is "good and acceptable and perfect." These three wonderful words should fill us all with confidence. So let's take a look at them.

> *What the Father envisions for your life is good, acceptable, and perfect.*

First, God's will is *good*. The Lord's plan is morally honorable, excellent, and beneficial to you. It may not always appear to be so at first. There have been times in my own life when I told the Father that the trials and pressures He was allowing seemed far from good. However, we always have to remember the promise of Romans 8:28: "We know that God causes all things to work together for good to those who love God, to those who are called according to His purpose." The Father is very careful about what He permits to touch your life. Why? Because He Himself is good. Psalm

145:8–9 affirms, "The LORD is gracious and merciful; slow to anger and great in lovingkindness. The LORD is good to all." Why would we ever expect the will of God to be anything other than good when both the nature and character of our heavenly Father are good?

Second, the Lord's plan for you is *acceptable.* It is both well pleasing to God but also satisfying to you. I believe this is an area where many believers struggle. We wrestle with how the Father views us and whether or not we are pursuing the best course of action in His sight. I have found this is especially true in Christians who grew up in very strict and/or critical households, who felt they could never meet the vague and unforgiving standards ever before them. If finding acceptance and worth is so difficult with people, how can we ever hope to measure up to God, Who is faultless in all His ways? But understand that the Lord receives you on the basis of what Jesus did on the cross. Once you have received Christ as your Savior, you are accepted before the Father forever. And because of the presence of the Holy Spirit in you and the Word of God to guide you, you can live in a manner well pleasing to the Lord. In fact, Philippians 2:13 asserts: "It is God who is at work in you, both to will and to work for His good pleasure." The Father patiently teaches you how to walk with Him—leading you along the way. So not only is it possible to live in an acceptable manner before Him, but God is committed to helping you do so, too!

> *Not only is it possible to live in an acceptable manner before Him, but God is committed to helping you do so, too!*

Third, and finally, God's will for you is *perfect.* When we read the word *perfect,* we may be daunted by thoughts of having to maintain a flawless walk with the Lord, but that is not what is intended by the word there. The Greek word *teleios* that is used is better translated as *finished, brought*

to maturity, enabled to reach the goal, or *needing nothing for completeness.*
Friend, the Father has no half-baked schemes—especially when it comes
to your life. You may not know His full plan, but He does. In fact, He knows
"the end from the beginning" (Isa. 46:10), and He can and will bring it to absolute completion. So there is never a need to worry about whether or not
God's plans will work out.

Staying on the Altar

The Lord's will is good, acceptable, and perfect. Why wouldn't anyone want
to serve a God like that? Certainly, there may—in the midst of walking with
Him—be difficult circumstances that are both confusing and painful. But
as I said in the beginning of this chapter, do not fear and do not despair.
Don't run from God because your situation is challenging—you may race
right out of His will, which is the worst choice you could make.

Rather, as Paul writes, "Do not be conformed." This is a command:
Fight the pattern of this world that would make you turn to your own resources rather than trust God. Likewise, "present your bodies a living
and holy sacrifice . . . be transformed by the renewing of your mind"
(Rom. 12:1–2). Set your will to allowing Jesus to work in your mind,
heart, and life. Give Him everything you are and hope to be. Invite the
Holy Spirit to change you into Christ's image—to tear down the old way
of thinking so the new can grow.

Of course, we all know that the problem with living sacrifices is that
they keep escaping from the altar. Presenting your total being—body, soul,
mind, spirit, will, desires, and emotion—completely to God is never easy. In
fact, there's nothing more challenging in life than that. I suspect that all of
us can say, "Lord, I've given myself to You as a sacrifice several times, but it
seems that as soon as I set my heart to serving You with everything I am,

something arises that I crawl off again. I give You my life, then immediately take it back."

Friend, this is not a onetime experience in life. I wish it were. I wish there was a way we could present ourselves to God once and that would be it—we would never have the temptation to take ourselves back again. But that's not a reality of our fallen human nature or the world we live in. We can see this repeatedly throughout the Old Testament—in both individuals and nations. We know that even though Abraham walked with God for more than eight decades and had His promise of an heir, when he and Sarah had difficulty conceiving a child he turned to his own devices and made an awful mistake—using Hagar as a surrogate (Gen. 16). Likewise, the Israelites would repent repeatedly, pledging to maintain a right relationship with the Lord, but when things didn't work out the way they wanted they took pagan practices from other religions and faced terrible trouble for it (Ps. 106:35–43). In other words, they crawled off the altar and started handling things their own way.

So, too, you may fail in your faith. You may fall to the temptations of this world, take matters into your own hands, and crawl off the altar. You may mess up in offering yourself as a living sacrifice. Do not fall for the enemy's lie that the Father has rejected you forever because of it (1 John 1:9). Part of God's process of making you into Christ's image is helping you understand the unseen strongholds that are preventing you from giving Him full access to your life. He reveals an area of stubborn self-sufficiency in you and then sets about breaking your bondage to it.

"The godly may trip seven times, but they will get up again."
—Proverbs 24:16 NLT

So don't give up! Proverbs 24:16 instructs: "The godly may trip seven times, but they will get up again" (NLT).

This is the difference between the godly and the lost, those who have faith and those who are faithless, those who have a true relationship with God and those who don't—the ability to get up and get back on the altar.

As someone who knows Jesus as your Savior, you always have Someone to help you up after you have fallen. You always have forgiveness. You always have hope for a good future. Therefore, get up and steady yourself on God Himself. Get back on the altar by realizing that Jesus never lets go of you (John 10:28–29). And take heart that His good, acceptable, and perfect will is not just within your reach, but He is working it out in your life as you trust Him.

3

DETERMINED VERSUS DESIRED

Understanding God's Sovereignty and Our Free Will

When I am considering God's will, one of the questions I frequently run into is that of inevitability. Is it absolutely inescapable that the Lord's plan will be accomplished? This is an important question when considering God's will because, as I discussed in the previous chapter, we know that His purpose is to transform believers into the likeness of Christ (Rom. 8:29). However, we also realize that many who claim Jesus as their Savior never really bear His image in a manner that draws others to Him. So how much is up to the Lord and how much is up to us? Can we mess it up? Likewise, do we have a choice of what our lives can be? More specifically, how much of His plan will God actively impose on us, and how much will we be able to choose for ourselves?

No doubt this is on your mind as you consider the questions on your heart today. If the Lord is completely in control of everything, then does it really matter what you decide? Won't He fix whatever mistakes you make in the end? Or if it is up to you to make the decision, then how can you ever be sure you heard Him right?

These are the questions all of us face when seeking God's will—especially in terms of decisions that are very important to us. In fact, this has been a tremendous debate in theological circles for some time—people trying to make sense of what they can count on the Lord to do and what is up to us to accomplish. Sadly, this subject has spurred much discussion and even division in the church. Some of it is less than helpful because rather than spur us to loving intimacy with the Father, the debates have caused confusion, anger, and fear. In this, I am reminded of Paul's words to his son in the faith, Timothy: "Solemnly charge them in the presence of God not to wrangle about words, which is useless and leads to the ruin of the hearers" (2 Tim. 2:14)—or, as the New Living Translation tells us, "can ruin those who hear them."

So I am not going to approach the topics of the Lord's sovereignty or our free will in the usual way, which is generally more systematic and philosophical. Instead, I wish to talk about these concepts in a manner that you can apply directly to how you seek God's will. So I will describe the two major aspects of the Lord's plan—that which He has *determined* will happen and that which He *desires* to happen.

God's Determined Will: Achieving His Sovereign Goals

The first aspect of God's plan we will look at is His *determined will*, which is the Lord's operation in the world—or how He operates as the Sovereign of the universe. Psalm 103:19 tells us: "The LORD has established His throne in the heavens, and His sovereignty rules over all." He is in control of all things. Any aspect of this universe He desires to influence He can. We must begin with this foundation because it is the basis for understanding how God keeps His promises.

✦ "The LORD of hosts has sworn saying, 'Surely, just as I have intended so it has happened, and just as I have planned so it will stand'" (Isa. 14:24).

✦ "I am God, and there is no one like Me, declaring the end from the beginning, and from ancient times things which have not been done, saying, 'My purpose will be established, and I will accomplish all My good pleasure' . . . . Truly I have spoken; truly I will bring it to pass. I have planned it, surely I will do it" (Isa. 46:9–11).

✦ "So will My word be which goes forth from My mouth; it will not return to Me empty, without accomplishing what I desire, and without succeeding in the matter for which I sent it" (Isa. 55:11).

The Lord is able to make these declarations because it is fully within His ability to accomplish anything that He says will come to pass. So God's *determined* or *sovereign* will is what will absolutely be done, regardless of what obstacles arise or what we do.

> *God's* determined *or* sovereign *will is what will absolutely be done.*

For example, as we saw in the first chapter, the Lord God promised to send us a Savior (Jer. 31:31–34). He faithfully accomplished this, and did so with a detailed list of specifications—such as what family Jesus would belong to (Gen. 12:3, 49:10; 2 Sam. 7:16), where He would be born (Mic. 5:2), when He would live (Dan. 9:25–26), what He would do (Isa. 61), the location of His ministry (Isa. 9:1; Matt. 4:12–17); and how He would redeem us from our sins (Isa. 53).

In fact, throughout Scripture, the Lord has made a great deal of His *determined* will known. For instance, He has made several unconditional covenants that have revealed His plan:

+ **The Abrahamic Covenant.** God promised Abraham, "I will make you a great nation, and I will bless you, and make your name great; and so you shall be a blessing; and I will bless those who bless you, and the one who curses you I will curse. And in you all the families of the earth will be blessed" (Gen. 12:2–3). In this, the Lord revealed the platform for His activity on earth: Abraham's family, who would eventually become the people of Israel. And we know that it is true that all the families of the earth have been blessed through Abraham, because our Savior, Jesus, came through his line (Gal. 3:8). Indeed, Abraham is "the father of all who believe" (Rom. 4:11) and "it is those who are of faith who are sons of Abraham" (Gal. 3:7).

+ **The Land Covenant.** Likewise, God told Abraham, "To your descendants I have given this land, from the river of Egypt as far as the great river, the river Euphrates" (Gen. 15:18). In other words, the Lord promised the geographical territory of Israel to Abraham's offspring. This does not mean that the people of Israel would continually live in and rule that particular region—we know they have not. History tells us that the Israelites spent 430 years in Egypt (Exod. 12:40–41), that they were scattered throughout Assyria (2 Kings 17:22–23) and exiled in Babylon (2 Chron. 36:14–20), and that they would eventually be expelled from the region for nineteen centuries until they were reconstituted as the State of Israel on May 14, 1948 (Ezek. 36:24). No other nation in history has ever reclaimed their territory three times or come back into existence after being dispersed for nineteen centuries. But Israel was able to do so because it was not up to them to achieve this promise; rather, it was dependent upon the Lord's provision.

+ **The Davidic Covenant.** In 2 Samuel 7:8–16, the Lord promised that He would bestow a very special blessing on David's line. He said, "I will raise up your descendant after you, who will come forth from you, and I will establish his kingdom. . . . I will establish the throne of his kingdom forever. . . . Your house and your kingdom shall endure before Me forever; your throne shall be established forever" (vv. 12–13, 16). Of course, we know this will be absolutely fulfilled when Jesus comes back as the reigning King of kings and Lord of lords, Who defeats His enemies, and establishes His throne forever (Rev. 19:16—21:27).

These covenants are unconditional—God brings them about regardless of what we do or decide. Likewise, we know that there are other unconditional promises throughout Scripture that He either has or will accomplish. Some examples are:

+ "I will never again send another flood to destroy the earth" (Gen. 9:11). Regardless of humanity's goodness or wickedness, the world will never be wiped out by deluge again.

+ "Each one of us will give an account of himself to God" (Rom. 14:12). Everyone will stand before the Lord (Heb. 9:27)—whether that be for judgment (Rev. 20:11–15) or for rewards (2 Cor. 5:10).

+ "At the name of Jesus every knee will bow, of those who are in heaven and on earth and under the earth, and that every tongue will confess that Jesus Christ is Lord, to the glory of God the Father" (Phil. 2:10–11). Whether we believe in Jesus or not, all will bow in recognition of His rulership. We can do so voluntarily or we will be compelled to do so, but all will acknowledge that Christ is Lord.

So the qualities we can extrapolate from God's *determined* will are as follows:

+ It is **inevitable**—it *will* happen. You can count on it.

+ It is **immutable**—the Lord will not change His mind or His plan.

+ It is **irresistible**—there's no one who can alter, delay, or oppose what God has established.

+ It is **purposeful**—the Father has wonderful, important, everlasting reasons for all His *determined* plans. They are not based on emotion or destructive whims. Rather, God has the crucial goals of eternity in view.

+ It is **comprehensive**—the Lord considers and provides for every detail that you and I could think of and countless more that we could never imagine. We never have to worry that He has considered every contingency, because He has—and then some.

+ It is **unpredictable**. This may seem a surprising characteristic considering that God has revealed so much of His *determined* will in Scripture. However, we should never believe that we can figure Him out or anticipate *how* He will accomplish His objectives. As He reminds us in Isaiah 55:8–9: "My thoughts are not your thoughts, nor are your ways My ways . . . For as the heavens are higher than the earth, so are My ways higher than your ways and My thoughts than your thoughts."

So God's *determined* will is what He's going to do—His inevitable, unchangeable, unalterable, purposeful, comprehensive, and lofty plans that bring Him great glory and praise. And what you and I must understand is that He doesn't make such plans exclusively for world events or nations. Rather, He also makes such plans for individuals. He makes them for you.

Psalm 139:15–16 affirms: "My frame was not hidden from You, when I was made in secret, and skillfully wrought in the depths of the earth; your eyes have seen my unformed substance; and in Your book were all written the days that were ordained for me, when as yet there was not one of them." So we can know for certain that there are aspects of our lives that are part of God's *determined* will.

> *"My frame was not hidden from You, when I was made in secret, and skillfully wrought."*
> —*Psalm 139:15*

For example, Acts 17:26–27 tells us, "He made from one man every nation of mankind to live on all the face of the earth, having determined their appointed times and the boundaries of their habitation, that they would seek God." In other words, the Father chose where, when, and to whom you would be born. He created you, so He chose your personality, talents, and abilities.

Scripture tells us that there are some people chosen for the Lord's special service before they are even born. He told Jeremiah, "Before I formed you in the womb I knew you, and before you were born I consecrated you; I have appointed you a prophet to the nations." The same was true for John the Baptist. The angel Gabriel told John's father, Zacharias, "He will turn many of the sons of Israel back to the Lord their God. It is he who will go as a forerunner before Him . . . to make ready a people prepared for the Lord" (Luke 1:16–17). So there are people the Father has determined will serve Him.

But it isn't just biblical saints like Jeremiah and John whom God creates and equips for His purposes. As we saw in the last chapter, Ephesians 2:10 tells us, "We are His workmanship, created in Christ Jesus for good works, which God prepared beforehand so that we would walk in them." The Lord God actively prepares each of us for certain assignments and gives us unique gifts with which to make an impact on this world for His name's sake (1 Cor. 12:7). Whether or not we walk in them is something I will discuss in a moment. I know that personally, I could not have denied Jesus when He called me to serve Him. However, I've also met several people who were called to preach and teach God's Word who refused to submit to His plan—and they greatly regretted it because of the hole they always felt in their lives.

But what is necessary for you to understand is that there are certain aspects of your life that are part of God's sovereign, determined, unchangeable plan that *will* happen. Of course, this may raise questions for you—especially when thinking about the hardships you've experienced and even the unfortunate decisions you've made. Were *those* part of His will for you? And if He is all-powerful and wise, why does the Father allow any suffering at all? You realize that we live in a fallen world, but perhaps it seems as if the One Who redeems us could do more to protect those who believe in Him. Likewise, *how much* of the Lord's plan is inevitable, unchangeable, and irresistible? Does it really matter what you do or how you live? Is it all part of some omnipotent scheme He has created? Or do the choices you make matter?

God's Desired Will: Leaving Room for Our Love

This brings us to the second aspect of our study, which is God's *desired* or *permissive will*. This is where you and I live every day—in the decisions we must make and in what the Father wants to do in our lives on a personal level. Most likely, what you face today has something to do with a choice you must make and you wonder why there is a conflict in your heart concerning it. This is because the Lord's *desired* will is neither irresistible nor unconditional. Rather, God gives us choices so that we can exercise our free will in obeying

> *God's* desired *or* permissive will *is where you and I live every day—in the decisions we make and in what the Father accomplishes in us on a personal level.*

Him. He does so for the purpose of having a genuine, loving relationship with us. He also does so in order to test our hearts—seeing whether we truly acknowledge that He is God.

For example, think of Adam and Eve in the Garden of Eden. There was really only one rule they had to submit to and that was: "From any tree of the garden you may eat freely; but from the tree of the knowledge of good and evil you shall not eat" (Gen. 2:16–17). Why did the Father leave them with this one prohibition? For the simple reason that the Lord wanted to give them an opportunity to trust Him and respect His authority—and to express that freely through their obedience to His command. In their flesh, they wanted that fruit. This is something we can often do—we want the one thing that has been denied to us rather than enjoying everything that has been freely given. So in order for them to honor God, they had to choose to trust His instruction to them rather than the curiosity and yearning for the fruit they were experiencing.

Without free will, without a choice to make, Adam and Eve would merely have been under obligation to the Lord God—like slaves under compulsion or robots programmed to carry out certain tasks. Our loving heavenly Father is not honored by that. Rather, He is pleased and exalted when we obey Him because we know He is trustworthy, wise, and always acts in love toward us.

Likewise, from our personal experience we know it is easy to *say* we love someone, bear allegiance to that person, or trust him or her; but when it comes to putting that person's needs or desires over our own, it becomes far more difficult. However, as any soldier or parent knows, real love is sacrificial. We prove our love when we put the other's well-being above our own. As Jesus said, "Greater love has no one than this, that one lay down his life for his friends" (John 15:13).

Our choices show whether we love God or not—and what we truly believe about Him.

In a sense, the same is true for God. We say we believe in and love the Lord, but do we trust Him more than we do ourselves? Are we willing to obey Him out of reverence, because He is our Creator, Savior, and Lord? Our choices show whether we do or not. We either respond to Him in faith—

acknowledging He is God by saying yes to Him—or in rebellion, choosing our own imperfect wisdom above His. This is up to us and ultimately reveals what we truly believe about Him.

So God's *desired* will is His personal involvement in our lives every day, regardless of what is happening. It is His direction in our decisions and it is something we can and should most certainly seek out. In fact, in Colossians 1:9 Paul writes: "We have not ceased to pray for you and to ask that you may be filled with the knowledge of His will in all spiritual wisdom and understanding." That a person can be "filled with the knowledge of His will in all spiritual wisdom and understanding" suggests that it is something we can take hold of. And when you think about it, it would be completely outside of God's character to expect you to make a particular choice or do something and then refuse to reveal it to you.

Therefore, whereas the Lord's *determined* will is inevitable and unpredictable apart from what He has revealed in His Word, the Father's *desired* will for your life is knowable in the circumstances you experience. And it requires you to make a decision about Who He is to you. Of course, that does not mean God is going to reveal every detail of the next ten years to you. He does not operate that way, because He wants you connected to Him in an intimate relationship continuously (1 Thess. 5:17). But you can certainly know what He wants you to do in the choices that are before you. This is why the author of Hebrews offers this prayer: "Jesus our Lord, equip you in every good thing to do His will, working in us that which is pleasing in His sight" (13:20–22). God can work it in you and equip you for it fully. He will not keep it secret unless you refuse to seek Him (Jer. 29:13).

In fact, one of the principles we need to realize is that God has already made a great deal of His *desired* will known to us. So in this next section, we are going to look at the different aspects of His *desired* or *permissive* will and how we can walk in it. Because the truth of the matter is that there are times when we come upon crossroads and make decisions that we don't realize are setting the course of our lives. No matter how vigilant we are, we are simply blind to their significance or impact on us and others. But when we are walking with Christ, He always makes sure to direct us in the right way. There is no way to lose when you obey God.

> *There is no way to lose when you obey God.*

1. God's Universal Moral Laws Revealed in Scripture

The first aspect of God's *desired* will that has already been revealed to us is through the laws and principles He has stated in His Word that apply to everyone. Perhaps the most famous of these decrees are the Ten Commandments (Exod. 20):

1. We should never honor any deity but the One True God of the Bible, who has revealed Himself through the nation of Israel (vv. 2–3).

2. We should never make or worship any idols (vv. 4–6).

3. We should never misuse the Lord's name but always show Him reverence and respect (v. 7).

4. We should remember to keep the Sabbath day holy (vv. 8–11).

5. We should honor and respect our fathers and mothers (v. 12).

6. We should never commit murder (v. 13).

7. We should never commit adultery (v. 14).

8. We should never steal (v. 15).

9. We should never lie or give false evidence against others (v. 16).

10. And we should never be envious of others' possessions or relationships (v. 17).

These are issues we need not even pray about—we know they are *always* the Lord's desire for us. Of course, there are many others. In the Sermon on the Mount (Matt. 5–7) we learn how to treat one another:

+ We should be poor in spirit, gentle, merciful, pure in heart, and always seek to make peace (5:3–9).

+ We should not lose heart when we mourn or are persecuted because we will be comforted and our reward in heaven is great (5:4, 10–12).

+ We should not commit murder, engage in adultery, make false vows, seek revenge, be anxious about tomorrow, or live in judgment of others (5:21–42, 6:25–32, 7:1–6).

+ We should love our neighbors and our enemies as well (5:43–47, 7:12).

+ We should pray, fast, and serve God alone—seeking His kingdom and righteousness, looking to Him always, and obeying His Word (6:1–24, 33–34; 7:7–11, 24–27).

Likewise, we know that it is always God's *desired* will that:

+ We be saved (1 Tim. 2:3–4; 2 Pet. 3:9).

+ We be filled with the Spirit and walk according to His direction (Rom. 8:4; Gal. 5:16, 25; Eph. 5:18).

+ We be baptized (Mark 16:16; Acts 2:38, 10:48; Rom 6:3–4; Gal. 3:27).

+ We pray continually and give thanks in every situation (Deut. 4:29; 1 Chron. 16:10–11; Ps. 34:10, 105:4; 1 Thess. 5:17–18).

+ We be sanctified (John 17:17; Rom. 6:19; 1 Thess. 4:3–7; Heb. 12:14).

+ We serve the Lord (Deut. 10:20; Ps. 100:2; Eph. 2:10, 6:7; Col. 3:23–24).

+ We tell others about Jesus and teach them to follow Him (Matt. 28:19–20; Mark 16:15; 2 Tim. 4:2).

+ We take part in His great plan to proclaim the gospel to every person in every nation, tribe, and tongue, to the ends of the earth (Matt. 24:14; Acts 1:8; Rev. 5:9, 7:9).

+ We faithfully fulfill our important part in the Body of Christ, edifying others with the gifts God has given us (1 Cor. 12:4–11; 1 Pet. 4:10).

+ We flee from all sexual immorality (1 Cor. 6:18; Eph. 5:3; Col. 3:5; 1 Thess. 4:3–5; 2 Tim. 2:22).

✦ We tithe and, indeed, entrust *all* we have to the God Who gave it to us (Lev. 27:30; Deut. 14:22; Mal. 3:10; Mark 12:41–44; Luke 6:38, 14:27–33; 2 Cor. 9:6–8; 1 Tim. 6:17–19).

✦ We forgive freely as Christ forgave us (Matt. 6:14–15; Eph. 4:32).

As I said, you do not need to ask God if it is His will that you be saved or baptized or forgive others. These actions are so powerfully and resolutely affirmed in His Word that we can know for certain they *are* His *desired* will for us.

But perhaps you are wondering why I would point out all of these commands in Scripture to you. After all, because of Christ's death on the cross, we're no longer judged by these laws (Gal. 4:5). He has paid our sin debt in full and we are under His forgiveness and grace (Gal. 5:18). So what does this mean for us?

The apostle Paul even asked, "What then? Shall we sin because we are not under law but under grace?" This can become our thinking. If Jesus forgives us of all our sins—past, present, and future—do we really need to obey the Word? Aren't we free from the demands of Scripture? But Paul immediately answers his own question emphatically: "May it never be!" (Rom. 6:15). So what is our responsibility in regard to these commands? Should they still be important to us?

Thankfully, Paul addresses this topic, because it is so crucial for us as believers. He writes:

Dear brothers and sisters—you who are familiar with the law—don't you know that the law applies only while a person is living? For example, when a woman marries, the law binds her to her husband as long as he is alive. But if he dies, the laws of marriage no longer apply to her. So while her husband is alive, she would be committing adultery if she married another man. But if her husband dies, she is free from that law and does not commit adultery when she remarries (Rom. 7:1–3).

Paul gives us a fantastic point of reference in order to understand our new relationship with the decrees of God's Word when we trust in Christ—and that is marriage. Paul explains that before we receive Jesus as our Savior we are related to the law as a wife is to her husband—tied by a contract that is dissolved only through death. The law is a difficult spouse—relentless in its demand for perfection.

Perhaps you've been around someone who was so put together that he or she made you feel like you could never measure up. It's not anything that person does or says that makes you feel inadequate; it's just that whenever you're around him or her, you realize how far you fall short. You are convicted about the wickedness of your thoughts, the inappropriateness of your actions, and even how unsuitable your eating habits are.

That's the law. Before Jesus, it is always with us—reminding us repeatedly how we fall short of God's perfect holiness—not just outwardly, but spiritually as well. After all, as Paul said, "I would not have come to know sin except through the Law; for I would not have known about coveting if the Law had not said, 'You shall not covet'" (Rom. 7:7).

Sadly, though the law could reveal our fallenness, it was powerless to change us in any way that truly mattered. It could not set us free from our sin, inadequacies, bondage, and imperfections. It could only remind us that what we can do is never enough—we can never save ourselves.

But then we meet Jesus—and *everything* about our new relationship with Him is good news! Paul tells us: "So, my dear brothers and sisters, this is the point: You died to the power of the law when you died with Christ. And now you are united with the One who rose from the dead. As a result, we can produce a harvest of good deeds for God" (Rom. 7:4). In other words, we die to sin when we accept Christ as our Savior, and Jesus makes us spiritually alive and able to live a life that's pleasing to Him (Rom. 6:11).

> *Jesus makes us spiritually alive and able to live a life that's pleasing to Him.*

Even better, Jesus is able "to keep you from stumbling and to present you before [the Father's] glorious presence without fault and with great joy" (Jude 24–25 NIV). You don't have to be perfect because Jesus—the sinless Son of God—has been perfect on your behalf. And how does He keep you from stumbling? He makes you into a new creation—one with the ability to walk in His will. As 2 Corinthians 5:17 assures us, "If anyone is in Christ, he is a new creature; the old things passed away; behold, new things have come."

Now that you are united with Jesus and no longer bound to the law—your death to sin has canceled your contract with it and broken its power over you. So then, what is your new relationship with the law? If the law is like a deceased spouse to us, does it have any bearing on our lives? Interestingly, the Sadducees asked Jesus a similar question. They said:

> "Teacher, Moses said, 'If a man dies having no children, his brother as next of kin shall marry his wife, and raise up children for his brother.' Now there were seven brothers . . . and the first married and died, and having no children left his wife to his brother; so also the second, and the third, down to the seventh.

Last of all, the woman died. In the resurrection, therefore, whose wife of the seven will she be? For they all had married her" (Matt. 22:24–28).

Of course, the Sadducees were debating an issue of Levitical law in order to trap the Savior. However, Jesus took the opportunity to teach a greater principle. He answered, "In the resurrection they neither marry nor are given in marriage, but are like angels in heaven" (Matt. 22:30). Of course, the only marriage in heaven is that we are the Bride of Christ (Eph. 5:25, 31–32; Rev. 19:7–8). But what Jesus said tells us a great deal about how we are now related to the law—it is like an angel of heaven to us. We know that the word for *angel*—in Hebrew *malak* and in Greek *angelos*—means "messenger" or "representative" in both languages. And throughout Scripture we see angels carrying out specific tasks for the Lord:

+ Delivering God's messages (Dan. 9:20–23; Matt. 28:5–7; Luke 1:13–17, 30–33, 2:10–14; Rev. 14:6–8).

+ Protecting God's people (Exod. 14:19–20; 2 Kings 6:11–17, 19:35; Ps. 34:7; Dan. 6:22).

+ Carrying out God's judgment on sin (2 Sam. 24:15–16; Isa. 6:5–7; Matt. 13:49; Rev. 8–9, 15:1).

+ Doing God's will, whatever it might be (Gen. 3:24; 1 Kings 19:1–8; Luke 22:43; John 5:4; Rev. 7:1, 20:1–3).

+ And leading in worship (Isa. 6:2–3; Rev. 5:11–14, 7:11–12).

This is a parallel to what the law—and indeed all of the Bible—is to us now. It no longer condemns us, but it does bring us closer to God and leads us in doing His *desired* will. Scripture can and should:

+ **Deliver God's message to us.** As we read the Bible, the Holy Spirit speaks to us and shows us what to do through it. He answers our questions, shows us what step to take next, and gives us understanding. This is why Psalm 119:105 says, "Your word is a lamp to my feet and a light to my path." We know the route of the Lord's plan because He reveals it to us through Scripture. As He tells us in Jeremiah 33:3: "Call to Me and I will answer you, and I will tell you great and mighty things, which you do not know."

+ **Protect us.** Throughout His Word, God is clear—His commands are meant to safeguard us and shield us from danger (Ps. 18:30). You see, at times we may think something is a grand idea because we do not perceive the dangers associated with it (Prov. 14:12). In our limited understanding, we may see something or someone we want and we cannot imagine why our yearnings could be destructive. But God does. Take adultery for example. It is disheartening to see how people get caught up in their lust for another person and don't consider the devastating consequences of violating their marriage vows. However, Proverbs compares it to scooping fire into one's lap (6:27) and warns: "The one who commits adultery with a woman is lacking sense; he who would destroy himself does it" (6:32). This is not the Father's desire for anyone—He doesn't want you to destroy yourself;

rather, He wants you to reach your full potential. So God's commands are not meant to prevent us from enjoying life.

On the contrary, they are meant to lead us to life at its very best. This is why the Lord told Joshua, "Be careful to do according to all the law which Moses

God's commands are meant to lead us to life at its very best.

My servant commanded you; do not turn from it to the right or to the left, so that you may have success wherever you go" (Josh. 1:7).

✦ ***Carries out God's judgment on sin.*** If there is anything that can identify, convict us of, and uproot sin in our lives, it is the Holy Spirit working through Scripture. Hebrews 4:12 tells us: "The word of God is living and active and sharper than any two-edged sword, and piercing as far as the division of soul and spirit, of both joints and marrow, and able to judge the thoughts and intentions of the heart." Whereas while we were spiritually dead the Word could only show us our faults (Rom. 7:7), because we are spiritually alive in Christ and in communion with the Lord it becomes our weapon to purge sin from our hearts (2 Cor. 10:5). In other words, through Scripture the Holy Spirit reveals not only the sin we are committing but also the consequences it is producing, why it has such a hold on us, and the root of error causing it. With such understanding—and the knowledge of our true identity in Christ we find in the Bible—we are equipped to win a lasting victory over the bondage.

✦ **Accomplishes God's will in our lives.** Throughout the Bible, we see angels doing various activities in obedience to the Lord: guarding what is sacred, feeding and nourishing the weary, comforting and strengthening those who struggle or mourn, bringing healing, and so forth. This is what His Word does in us as well. Paul wrote: "All Scripture is inspired by God and profitable for teaching, for reproof, for correction, for training in righteousness; so that the man of God may be adequate, equipped for every good work" (2 Tim. 3:16–17). It is amazing how the Father will bring to mind the perfect verse when you are hurting, counseling others, need wisdom, or require encouragement to endure difficult circumstances. The Holy Spirit works through Scripture to reveal Himself, teach us how to walk with Him, conform us to Christ's image, and minister to others.

✦ **Leads us to worship Him.** Have you ever been reading the Word and the Holy Spirit touched such a profound place within you and spoke to your heart in such a powerful way that you began to worship God because of His awesome goodness to you? We see this when the scribe named Ezra opened God's Word and began to read it to the people in Jerusalem: "Ezra opened the book in the sight of all the people . . . Then Ezra blessed the LORD the great God. And all the people answered, 'Amen, Amen!' while lifting up their hands; then they bowed low and worshiped the LORD with their faces to the ground" (Neh. 8:5–6). Ezra read the Word to them in a manner they could understand (v. 8), and at first this caused them to weep because they realized that they had sinned and failed to serve the Lord in a manner worthy of His name (v. 9). But then, when they realized God's provision to them, they rejoiced. "All the people went away to . . . celebrate a great festival, because they understood the words which had been made known to them" (v. 11). At times, we come before the Lord and it's possible we're not really certain of what is causing us the internal discomfort we live with. Then He reveals our sin and gives us an opportunity to repent. When we do, we suddenly feel the release of all that internal static. This, in turn, leads us to understand how deeply God is providing for us in the issues closest to our hearts. It is an awesome moment of feeling so completely loved and cared for—understanding how profoundly

God speaks directly to our most intimate needs and can answer the deepest questions of our souls through His Word.

He works on our behalf. It is in those moments that He speaks directly to our most intimate needs and can answer the deepest questions of our souls through His Word. If you have never experienced that, I pray the Lord will open up Scripture to you in that way. Because God's Word reveals Who He is and how much He loves you in a manner nothing else can.

That is what Scripture can do and how God uses it to reveal His *desired* will to us. You come to know His truth and respond in obedience to it—and what is the result? "The truth will make you free" (John 8:32). So we see that before salvation, God's Word can only point to your need *for* the

Lord. But after salvation, Scripture also reveals your absolute freedom *through* the Lord—through what Jesus has done for you and what He has planned for you.

So what are the consequences when we do not follow God's moral law? Often this is when we experience suffering—when either we or others refuse to obey the Lord. That's not always the case, of course. But others may hurt us and make life very difficult for us. Or people may set off a chain of events in their sinfulness that lead to disastrous consequences that affect your life. Does God *cause* those circumstances? No. They are not necessarily a part of His *determined* will for you. And we know for certain that sin *never* originates with the Lord. Sin is utterly inconsistent with His character. The entire testimony of Scripture is clear: He is holy and everything He does is good, just, and righteous (Lev. 19:2; James 1:13). In fact, the reason Jesus could take our sin upon Himself is because He was completely blameless—absolutely sinless and perfectly holy (2 Cor. 5:21). So then why does He allow others' sinful actions to affect us?

Friend, if your heavenly Father perceives some redemptive value in a problem that threatens to touch your life—if He can work something positive out of it for you—He will permit it.

We saw this when we looked at Romans 8:28: "We know that God causes all things to work together for good to those who love God, to those who are called according to His purpose." That means that out of 100 difficulties in your life, it is not only 50, or 75, or even 99 that will ultimately benefit you if you trust Him. Rather, all 100 will work together for your good.

> *Of 100 difficulties, God will work all 100 together for good in your life.*

But take heart in the converse fact as well: If God *does not* perceive any redemptive value in trouble that is headed your way, He protects you from it. Lamentations 3:33 affirms, "He does not afflict willingly or grieve the sons of men." At times, we do not realize that things could be far worse for us, but our kind and loving Lord does indeed shield us in ways that would defy imagination.

2. God's Planned Intentions for Your Life

But this concept of the Father working all things together for our good leads to the second area of God's desires we'll look at, which is *His planned intentions for our lives*. After all, the Father has given us spiritual gifts by which to serve and He has equipped us to accomplish His objectives. He makes plans for our vocations, whom we marry, whom we will inspire, and the impact He desires for us to make on the world through our testimonies. So the Father may provide influences around us that steer us in the direction of a particular way of life or field of service.

For example, the Lord may put teachers or mentors on your path who help bring out a particular interest or talent that is within you. Or He may allow a difficult situation that develops wisdom and a particular set of graces in you—opening up an unexpected ministry field to you.

I have often spoken of a Sunday school teacher named Craig Stowe, who made a fantastic difference in my life. He told our Bible class a story about being in the U.S. Navy during World War II that I will never forget. As you can imagine, we boys were all ears as he told of enemy vessels approaching our brave American forces and threatening attack. As the crewmen of his ship were readying themselves for the battle, the commander asked for a volunteer to go up on the crow's nest—which was dizzyingly high on the mainmast—to act as a lookout for the inbound adversarial forces. This post was crucial, of course; however, it was also very dangerous and terrifying—and everyone knew it. Not only was the crow's nest incredibly far off the ground, but it also offered little protection against incoming fire. Anyone up there would be an easy target. As might be expected, no one came forward to volunteer.

But Craig told us that the Lord spoke to him clearly and assured him, "Craig, I'm with you just as much up there as I am down here. You can do it." So he stepped out in faith and agreed to take on the harrowing task. Though the attack was fierce and many men were lost, Craig came through the battle without even a scratch. He told us, "Nothing ever came anywhere near me. God protected me, just as He promised."

All these years later, I still remember my Sunday school teacher Craig Stowe and how the Lord was with him up on that crow's nest. He was the only man I can remember during my youth who truly showed he cared for me, and his example of courage inspired me so much that I wanted to be just like him. In fact, I've recalled his story many times when I've had to make decisions and take on tasks that frightened me. Thinking about him always reminds me that God will always be with me, too—regardless of where I am or what enemy fire might come my way. So the Father used Craig in a powerful way to influence me to take on some assignments and ministry positions I may not have taken otherwise.

> *God will always be with me—regardless of where I am or what enemy fire might come my way.*

Certainly, there are people in your life who have influenced your direction as well. But perhaps there are also difficult circumstances that have shaped who you are and how you see things. This is undoubtedly true for me. My father passed away when I was merely nine months old, so my mother was the sole breadwinner for our family. This meant that I was alone a great deal of the time when I was young, because my mother had to work long hours to support us. Eventually, my mother married John Hall, a very negative man whom she'd met at the Dan River Mills, where she worked. Hostility and conflict seemed to follow John wherever he went. I had terrible arguments with him and I never really felt safe when he was around. So I tried to be away from our house as often as possible.

One place I would go was to the church—down to the basement area, in the quietest, darkest, most remote Sunday school classroom I could find. I loved it because I could pray all I wanted to—as loudly and for however long I needed to. During those times, it was just me and God, and I spent many very meaningful hours with Him without any distractions. I would ask Him to show me Who He was, how I could know Him better, what I could do to serve Him, and how I could accomplish His will. So even though my home life had negative aspects to it, I will always be grateful for the life-long habit of prayer that developed because of it, which has shaped my life and ministry. So in this as well, the Father worked through my circumstances to carry out His planned intention for my life: that I would rely on my relationship with Him through prayer for every decision I would make.

Of course, I have just given you two instances where the Lord's influence was received in a positive manner—where His direction achieved results and His *desired* will was accomplished. However, we should not lose sight that we must respond in obedience to Him in order for that to be true. Throughout Scripture we see that there is room for us to decide whether or not to join Him in His work.

For example, perhaps you recall the account of the rich young ruler (Matt. 19:19–26). He asked Jesus how he could have eternal life. The young man, of course, was thinking of going to heaven, as most would. But Jesus surprised him when He replied, "If you wish to be complete, go and sell your possessions and give to the poor, and you will have treasure in heaven; and come, follow Me" (v. 21). You see, Jesus defines eternal life differently than we might. Certainly, going to heaven is part of it. But Jesus says, "This is eternal life, that they may know You, the only true God, and Jesus Christ whom You have sent" (John 17:3). Eternal life is about a relationship with the Lord that starts right now. In other words, Jesus was telling that young man, "Know Me. Join Me. Make the Lord God your God above everything else in your life." His instruction to the rich young ruler of selling all his possessions was not meant to be a checklist for earning salvation; rather, it was the real choice before him—would he serve God or money?

Unfortunately, verse 22 tells us that the young man "went away grieving; for he was one who owned much property." So we see that there are people called to know and serve God who refuse to do so.

Likewise, sometimes people serve the Lord, but not wholeheartedly. For example, when the armies of Aram threatened to attack Israel, King Joash went to see the prophet Elisha for wisdom about how to proceed against such a formidable foe. Elisha told Joash to shoot his arrows out of the eastern window, because, he proclaimed, "This is the LORD's arrow, an arrow of victory over Aram . . . Now pick up the other arrows and strike them against the ground" (2 Kings 13:17–18 NLT). In other words, Elijah challenged Joash to shoot the arrows out of the window and into the earth as a sign of his trust that God would win the battle. Sadly, Joash shot only three of the arrows and held the rest back, demonstrating that he didn't really believe the Lord's provision. And because of his lack of faith, he failed to achieve a complete victory over the enemy armies.

So God's *desired* will is that we serve Him—and that we do so wholeheartedly. Whether we do and to the extent that we do is up to us.

> God's desired *will is that we serve Him— and that we do so wholeheartedly. Whether we do and to the extent that we do is up to us.*

Now, sometimes the Lord will chase you down until you obey Him— as He did with the prophet Jonah. As you may recall, Jonah was tasked with preaching to the ruthless Ninevites, who were bitter enemies of Israel. Nineveh was the capital of Assyria at the time and approximately five hundred miles northeast of Jerusalem.

The Lord said, "Arise, go to Nineveh the great city and cry against it, for their wickedness has come up before Me" (Jonah 1:2). God was going to judge Nineveh and wipe it out unless its people repented (3:2–4). Out of compassion for them, the Lord wanted His prophet Jonah to let them know how their situation had deteriorated (4:11). But because of his hatred for the Ninevites, Jonah ran from the assignment. In fact, Jonah, ran the opposite direction to Tarshish, which was approximately 2,500 miles west of Jerusalem. He got as far away from Nineveh as he could.

What this shows us is that though God wanted Jonah to preach to the Ninevites, Jonah did have free will to run away. He was not a robot who automatically did what the Lord wanted. However, it also shows us that running away from God doesn't release us from His commands. We are still accountable for what He has created us to do—especially because others' lives may be at stake.

We know that the Lord sent Jonah adversity—in the form of a terrible storm (1:4–16) and a large fish (1:17)—to get the prophet back on the right track. And eventually, Jonah repented and did as God asked (2:1–10). So God will pursue you in order for His *planned intentions* for your life to be accomplished.

The very best path is always to obey God immediately—because disobedience is always very costly.

However, don't be lured into erroneously thinking the Lord will chase you forever—that there is always time to repent and get back on track. This is not always the case. God's awesome grace gives you second chances, but the very best path is always to obey Him immediately. Why? Because your disobedience is always costly—to both you and those around you. It certainly was for Jonah. When you flee from the Father, not only are you leaving your peace and joy behind because He is the true Source of them, but you may be hampering the eternal goals He desires to accomplish through you. Disobedience certainly deprives you of the joy of your reward.

3. God's Plan for When We Make Mistakes

Of course, you may be wondering, *What if I don't realize what God's will is or if I make a mistake in obeying Him? What if I simply fail? What then? Have I ruined my life forever?* This is a topic that can haunt even the strongest heart. We think of the things we have done wrong throughout our lives and question if they have disqualified us from experiencing His best for us.

So the next the aspect of the Father's *desired* will I'm going to discuss is *when we make mistakes*. What happens to His will when we mess up? Because the truth of the matter is no one, other than Jesus, can say he or she has always done God's will—certainly, I cannot. We act in ignorance. We rebel. We fail. And at times, the errors we commit are excruciatingly painful, are financially, relationally, or physically costly, and send us into a spiral of discouragement that is difficult to overcome.

But no matter where you are, what you have done, or who you've hurt—whatever the mistake—when you acknowledge that you were wrong, you repent of your sins, and you submit yourself to God, He sets in motion a plan for you to get back on track. This does not necessarily mean that you get back on the path of His *original* will for you. If God calls you to preach when you are nine years old, but you ignore Him until you are ninety, naturally you will not be able to experience or accomplish all He initially intended for you.

However, it doesn't matter if you are nine, nineteen, or ninety-nine—your heavenly Father always has a *circumstantial* plan for you—

God picks up the broken pieces of your life, and with the glue of His love and forgiveness He puts you back together and gives you a wonderful purpose.

assignments for you to fulfill on your particular place on the path. He picks up the broken pieces of your life, and with the glue of His love and forgiveness He puts you back together and gives you a wonderful purpose.

So you're telling me that the Father can restore and work through anyone? That He can bring joy and meaning back to my life? That He can heal me of all these regrets?

Absolutely He can. You may feel low about yourself, but we all need Christ's forgiveness—and He is very willing to forgive (1 John 1:9). After all, remember what Paul said about himself: "Jesus came into the world to save sinners—of whom I am the worst" (1 Tim. 1:15 NIV). Why did Paul think of himself in this way? Because he had persecuted the church, punishing those who followed Jesus. To him, there could be no worse crime than attacking the people and work of God.

Yet Paul also said this: "God had mercy on me so that Christ Jesus could use me as a prime example of His great patience with even the worst sinners" (1 Tim. 1:16 NLT). Paul is saying that when you feel low about yourself you can look at the mercy and grace Jesus showed him and realize that Christ can turn your life around, too. What is necessary, however, is that you take on the apostle Paul's attitude: "Forgetting what lies behind and reaching forward to what lies ahead, I press on toward the goal for the prize of the upward call of God in Christ Jesus" (Phil. 3:13–14). After you receive Christ's forgiveness, not only is it imperative to forgive yourself of your past regrets and forget them, but you must also leave behind your former ways of behaving and thinking that led to those mistakes.

Friend, understand the Lord's attitude toward you, which is reflected in the actions of the father in the Parable of the Prodigal Son (Luke 15:11–32). Perhaps you remember this story about a young, headstrong man who asked his father for his share of the inheritance—implying his father was dead to him. This young man left home, wasted his money, and found himself in deep destitution.

The father in the parable never gave up on his son—just like your heavenly Father never gives up on you. Yes, God's heart is grieved when you turn away from Him to pursue your own agenda and desires. But the reason your departure saddens Him is because He understands that when you run from Him and live in sin it can only lead you to increasing disillusionment and despair. So like the father in the story, He watches you and waits for you to realize that what you're doing isn't working.

> *Your heavenly Father watches you and waits for you to realize that what you're doing isn't working.*

Eventually, when the prodigal returned home, the father saw him while he was still a long way off and ran to meet him. Instead of berating him or saying, "I told you so," that dad felt compassion for his boy—he embraced him and showed him unconditional love. In the same way, the heavenly Father forgives and welcomes us home when we repent of our sin and return to Him.

That may seem almost too easy to some people—shouldn't there be a greater price for our sins? But recognize that along the way, the prodigal son lost valuable time and resources—in fact, he lost his earthly inheritance. Those were not restored to him, because disobedience is costly.

Thankfully, because of his father's great love, he still had a future. And so do you.

I heard about an awesome example of this at the seminary I graduated from as a young man, Southwestern Baptist Theological Seminary. It came to the attention of the school that there were men on death row who had accepted Christ as their Savior and who now wanted to serve Him in some manner, even though they were confined to life in prison. Of course, if anyone might consider themselves disqualified from God's service it would be a man who was deemed so dangerous to society that he would be locked up for the rest of his life. But instead of counting those men out, the seminary professors believed that God was revealing a unique opportunity to train a new kind of missionary.

Southwestern Seminary began offering a four-year degree to inmates who would make the prison their mission field and who would preach the gospel to those confined with them. In this way, God opened up an incredible opportunity for those inmates to serve Him, proving once again that the Holy Spirit can work through anyone who is willing to obey the Lord. Those men found His awesome purpose for their lives and for their difficult circumstances. And let me tell you, it has revolutionized that detention facility and the lives of countless men. As of 2018, 180 graduates have become ministers at twenty-six prisons[2]—turning places once reserved for the walking dead into sanctuaries of God's grace where people are actively learning about new life in Christ.

Your heavenly Father can always make a way. Sadly, the devil has tricked some believers into thinking that the Lord cannot work through them anymore. That they are too old, defiled, or backward for Him to shine His wonderful light and love through their lives. But nothing could be further from the truth.

God has always used imperfect people for His awesome purposes. He specializes in taking broken lives and turning them into joyful, productive, and inspiring trophies of His grace. That is the supernatural, unfailing

[2] https://www.houstonchronicle.com/news/houston-texas/houston/article/Texas-prison-TDCJ-seminary-baptist-minister-12895540.php.

power of the gospel! Christ can take any person, anywhere, with any past and forgive them, change their hearts, give them a new sense of direction, and work through them for His glory. So always have faith that Jesus will pick you up and restore you right where you are.

> *God specializes in taking broken lives and turning them into joyful, productive, and inspiring trophies of His grace.*

4. God's Daily Activity in Your Life—His Immediate Will

Ultimately, the place to start getting on the path of God's *desired* will for your life is in your daily walk with Him. This is where you can see how intimately involved He is with every detail that concerns you. You begin to connect how He is moving and how He prompts you to do His will.

You can experience this through your quiet time in the morning, which I will talk about in the next chapter. You read God's Word and there is a passage of Scripture that stands out to you. Then, as you go about your day, you encounter a situation where that verse is helpful to you. For example, it may be that you read Ephesians 4:32, which says: "Be kind to one another, tender-hearted, forgiving each other, just as God in Christ also has forgiven you." You have that verse on your mind and in your heart as you encounter a coworker who is in a foul mood and very rude to you. Wanting to honor the Lord, you extend kindness to that person and discover his or her terrible attitude is due to difficulties he or she is carrying by him- or herself. God turns a situation that could have resulted in an ugly conflict into an opportunity for ministry because you obey Him.

This can happen in many ways as God speaks to you through your daily Scripture reading. As we saw earlier in this chapter, He will bring verses to mind when you need comfort, renew your hope through the wonderful promises of His Word, give you direction, and convict you of sin.

But have you ever found that at times the Father will lead you to the same passage of Scripture over and over again? I recall an occasion when I was seeking the Lord's will about a decision, and I kept finding myself reading Isaiah 6:8: "Then I heard the voice of the Lord, saying, 'Whom shall I send, and who will go for Us?' Then I said, 'Here am I. Send me!'" It appeared in all sorts of different contexts throughout my day for several days—in my Bible reading and study, in different devotionals, on the radio, in correspondence from friends, you name it. I realized this was God showing me exactly what He wanted me to do, and when I finally said yes to the Lord, Isaiah 6:8 was no longer a prominent theme in my day.

This is the way the Father is revealing Himself to you and teaching you to be sensitive to His voice. Eventually, you realize that when you feel a particular tug on your heart or sense a restraint in your spirit, it is His Holy Spirit speaking to you. It could be that you are listening to a message and you sense the Father revealing specific steps of how you are to follow Him in obedience. It can also be that the Lord brings a person to mind and you feel that you should call him or her. When you do, you find that person needs encouragement and that your contact is actually a very real and powerful answer to his or her prayers.

These are all ways God prompts you to obey His *desired* will on a daily basis. He is speaking to your heart, warning you about danger, and encouraging you to submit to His purposes.

Of course, you may be doubtful. Does God really care about such small details? Absolutely He does! I have seen the Father do so many wonderful things that may seem insignificant to others but are very meaningful to me. I can't help but be utterly convinced of His participation in every aspect of our lives.

This is a simple example, but it illustrates the principle. I don't usually wear handkerchiefs, cuff links, or tie clips when I preach, because that isn't my style. I don't want the people watching to be distracted from the message. However, I do wear a particular wristwatch when I speak. It is not my everyday watch, but a special one a friend gave to me. I try to be extra careful with it because it is meaningful to me.

Not long ago, I was going on a long trip and I didn't want to take that watch with me for fear of losing or damaging it. So, in an effort to keep it safe, I hid it in my house. Well, when I got back home I couldn't find it. I looked for it for a couple of weeks.

Finally, I sat down in my office and prayed, "Father, I know that You know where that watch is. What did I do with it? Please show me. I need it."

At that moment, I was sitting at my desk and I suddenly got an inclination to look something up in my dictionary, which was on the shelf in front of me. And as I pulled the book out of its place, there it was—the watch I had been looking for. It had been just two feet away from me! Was that coincidence? Absolutely not.

Don't ignore the still, small, quiet ways that the Spirit of God speaks to your heart. Because as you submit to the promptings of the Holy Spirit, you recognize His voice more and more. Eventually, you begin to perceive and understand spiritual realities that only a person who is in constant communion with the Father can perceive. As Isaiah 30:21 says, "Your ears will hear a word behind you, 'This is the way, walk

> *Don't ignore the quiet ways the Spirit of God speaks to your heart, because He is teaching you to recognize His voice in increasing measure.*

in it,' whenever you turn to the right or to the left." So yield to the Holy Spirit—submit to His promptings and depend on His ability to direct you in the daily matters. He will teach you how to live a life that is pleasing to

Christ, and will also enable you to experience God in ways you never imagined possible.

Fully Invested

After this chapter, I pray you have a clearer understanding of both God's *determined* and *desired* will. Of course, we may not know for certain what parts of the Lord's will for us are His sovereign plan and which are His permissive plan until we get to heaven. I realize that in some ways this chapter may have stirred up even more questions for you—especially as you seek Him for the specific issues that are before you today.

As I said in the previous chapter, *do not be afraid*. The important thing for you to know is not whether the decision before you is His *determined* or *desired* will, but that He is *fully* invested in His *whole* plan. If you are seeking God and have a heart to do His will, you are promised that He *will* show you what to do. Jesus Himself said, "Ask, and it will be given to you; seek, and you will find; knock, and it will be opened to you. For everyone who asks receives, and he who seeks finds, and to him who knocks it will be opened" (Matt. 7:7–8). That is God's heart toward you. As your heavenly Father, He wants you to ask, seek, and knock so He can give, reveal, open, and provide what is good for you (Matt. 7:11).

That means that even when you are not clear about the choice to make—if for whatever reason He keeps His will concealed—you can take comfort in the fact that "it is God who is at work in you, both to will and to work for His good pleasure" (Phil. 2:13). The Lord takes responsibility for directing you through the fog. As I often say, He will move heaven and earth to show you His will. In the following chapter, we will look at some of the ways He does so.

But understand that you have everything you need in order to walk in His plan for your life—the Holy Spirit Who lives and works within you and His Word to direct you. He is constantly prompting you to remain in the center of His will and is faithful to adjust your path when you begin to drift—even when you don't realize it.

Therefore, you do not have to grieve or struggle to know God's will and you do not have to manipulate your circumstances to make His plan happen. Rather, employ your energy in exhibiting faith and walking step by step with Him, being confident that He is actively working in the unseen on your behalf (Isa. 64:4). Because you can be certain that when your heart is inclined toward Him, He uses all the resources at His disposal to accomplish what concerns you (Ps. 57:2).

> *When your heart is inclined toward God, He uses all the resources at His disposal to accomplish His will in your life.*

I realize this may not answer all your questions or calm all your fears. You may say, *I don't know if I really have confidence that God will help me. I really feel like I need an answer. I need to know what to do.* To this I say, "Wait for the LORD; be strong and let your heart take courage; yes, wait for the LORD" (Ps. 27:14). There are many aspects of your life that you entrust to others. You trust doctors with your health, financial advisors with your retirement, accountants with your taxes, and you send your children to teachers to receive an education. No matter how skilled and trustworthy these experts are, is not God even more so?

It is crucial for you to grasp how reliable the Father is to lead you, because you are making your choices based on what you believe. Sometimes we can count on the people involved in our choices; sometimes we can't.

At times, we know most of the facts surrounding our decisions, but usually we don't know everything. But you cannot judge God by those standards because He is so far above them.

The Lord your God is the only One Who has all the facts, Who knows the full truth, Who can guide you unwaveringly to what is right and good every time. He is the sovereign, omniscient God. He is the only One fully capable of accomplishing whatever He promises. He is going to have His way no matter what happens. Therefore, it is *always* wise to include the Lord in all your decision-making and to entrust Him with every aspect of your life.

So even when details of His plan remain mysterious to you—even when you don't understand what's going on or know what to do—trust Him and obey inch by inch and step by step. Choose to submit to and have faith in the God Who loves you unconditionally. He has the best plan for your life, has equipped you to accomplish it, and will enable you to fulfill all His awesome purposes for you as you walk with Him.

4

GOD WILL SHOW YOU HIS WILL

Components of the Discovery

I have said repeatedly throughout this book that not only does Christ have a plan for your life, but He also is faithful to reveal it to you. But how do you discover it? I realize that this is the most significant question I'll discuss when speaking about God's will. And now that I have laid the groundwork for understanding the Lord's purposes and ways, we can look at *how* the Father communicates His desires to us.

Because when it comes to our personal lives, yes, there are *determined* objectives the Lord will absolutely accomplish in and through us. However, for the most part, Jesus wants us to join Him out of love and obedience to His high and honorable purposes for our lives—or His *desired* will. As I've discussed, this is the very best path for us—what is good, acceptable, and perfect. God's plan is how we reach the maximum of our potential as individuals and how we take hold of the awesome fulfillment we're looking for and that our heavenly Father desires for us.

But in order for us to willingly participate in Christ's plan, we have to know what it is. We must be able to discern the way He wants us to take.

So what I have to show you in this chapter is absolutely crucial. And if you will keep each of the points I show you in the forefront of your thinking as you make decisions each day, you're going to discover the will of God much more easily and He will do awesome things in your life.

Because God *will* show you His plan when you seek Him. Decide right now to believe this simple fact—*your Savior wants you to know His will so you can walk in it.* How do I know this?

First, it is God's* character *to reveal His will to you. Think about it: If the Lord wants you to live a certain way and make specific choices, then He must assume responsibility for teaching you the right thing to do. He understands that the road can become confusing and that often the choices you face are difficult and complex. You are trying to figure out what is best for you—anticipating obstacles and opportunities you cannot see in a future that is unsure.

But as a good and faithful Father, Who does see what's ahead, He is more than willing to help you—and He says so *many* times in His Word. In Psalm 32:8, He assures you, "I will instruct you and teach you in the way which you should go; I will counsel you with My eye upon you." This is why you read about people such as David praying, "Teach me to do Your will, for You are my God; let Your good Spirit lead me on level ground" (Ps. 143:10). David knew this to be the Lord's character— that He wants us to know His will so we can walk in it (1 Chron. 16:8–12).

> *God assumes responsibility for teaching you His will so you can walk in it.*

This leads us to my second point, which is that God* promises *to show you His will. James 1:5 proclaims: "If any of you lacks wisdom, let him ask of God, who gives to all generously and without reproach, and it will be given to him." Likewise, Proverbs 28:5 affirms: "Those who seek the

LORD understand all things." In fact, throughout this book you have seen many times the Father has promised to reveal His plans to you. There are so many that I have included a list of promise verses about God's Will as an appendix for your encouragement.

But the point is that you can be absolutely certain the Lord will show you His will. As Psalm 16:11 asserts, "You will make known to me the path of life; in Your presence is fullness of joy; in Your right hand there are pleasures forever."

With this in mind, let's get started.

Communion with God Through Scripture

I am going to begin each of the following eight points about how to discover God's will with the letter *C* so that they will be easier to remember and implement in your life. However, I would suggest that you take a three-by-five card and write them down as you learn them—posting them in a place where you can review them often.

I recommend that at the very top and center of the card in large letters write: **"Communion with God Through Scripture."** At the bottom and center of the card in large letters write: **"Communication with God Through Prayer."** The reason for this is so that all of the other points are understood and acted upon in light of these two practices. If you want to know God's will, the Father will use your time in *communion* and *communication* with Him—through His Word

If you want to know God's will, the Father will use your time in communion and communication with Him—through His Word and in prayer—to show how everything you experience relates to His plan for your life.

and in prayer—to show how everything you experience relates to His plan for your life.

Of course, we already saw a great deal about how the Father speaks to us through His Word in the previous chapter. It is absolutely crucial to our walk with Him. And the reason we begin with God's Word now is because that is the best way to learn His voice, how He responds, and what He expects. But the Father also speaks to our particular situations in its pages. We know that He would never tell us anything that contradicts what He has written in Scripture. Through it, He teaches us what the Christian life should look like, what no longer fits us as His children, and how to avoid the pitfalls of life.

For example, 2 Timothy 3:16–17 tells us: "All Scripture is inspired by God and profitable for teaching, for reproof, for correction, for training in righteousness; so that the man of God may be adequate, equipped for every good work." In other words, the Bible speaks to what the Father desires for us to do and helps us to accomplish it. It is His instruction book for living. It is:

+ **Inspired.** Literally, Scripture is *God breathed*. This is how the Lord wrote the sixty-six books through His approximately forty servants throughout the ages—He divinely breathed them out, inspiring the authors through His Spirit to write them. The Bible did not originate with people; it came from His mind and its principles carry His power. Think about it. Many of the Old Testament authors probably did not realize the fullness of the prophecies they proclaimed—especially those about Jesus and the End Times—but only understood them in part (1 Pet. 1:10–12). This means it had to originate from a source outside them and, indeed, outside of time itself

(Isa. 46:10). And it means the Bible is like no other book in the world because it flowed from the heart of God rather than man. Thankfully, because this is true, the Holy Spirit can speak directly to your circumstances through it.

+ **Profitable.** The Word is helpful and advantageous to you. Scripture will always steer you toward God's will because it is His very thoughts toward us. How does it do so?

+ **Teaching.** Even if there is no one else around to instruct you, the Bible tells you about Jesus. It imparts truth about His ways, how to follow Him, and how to honor Him in the choices you face. But it also teaches you about yourself, others, how to have healthy relationships, and how to handle the situations of life such as conflicts, failures, and opportunities.

+ **Reproof.** The Bible is useful for helping you understand the attitudes, beliefs, and habits that are undermining your well-being and relationship with Christ. It is persuasive, convicting of you of where you are going wrong in thought or conduct so you can change course. This is what Jesus means in John 8:32: "You will know the truth, and the truth will make you free."

+ **Correction.** But not only does the Word convict you of wrongful attitudes and habits; it also helps you get on the *right* path. It restores you from the damage those erroneous thoughts and behaviors have caused you—actually improving your life and character and making you complete as a child of God.

✦ **Training in righteousness.** Likewise, the Holy Spirit does not leave us at a surface or elementary level of godliness. Rather, through Scripture, He trains us by renewing our minds, deepening our faith, healing our most profound strongholds, and transforms us into the image of Christ (Rom. 8:29, 12:1–2). It takes us further and deeper in the faith. As Hebrews 5:13–14 teaches us, "Everyone who partakes only of milk is not accustomed to the word of righteousness, for he is an infant. But solid food is for the mature, who because of practice have their senses trained to discern good and evil."

Remember the goal of all this: "So that the man of God"—and actually the word there is *anthropos*, which is better translated as the *human being* or *person of God*, so this applies to *everyone*—"may be adequate, equipped for every good work" (2 Tim. 3:17). This is all so you can fulfill the awesome purposes the Lord has created you to walk in. So that you can be:

✦ **Adequate**—complete and perfectly fit for the task. Often I hear people say that they are scared to do God's will because they do not feel suited for what the Lord is calling them to do. They are fearful of being proven weak, ineffectual, unworthy, or incapable. But what the Father does through His Word is to remind you of your new identity in Christ—that you are a beloved child of the almighty God (Rom. 8:16), born again to a living hope (1 Pet. 1:23), formed as His masterpiece (Ps. 139:13–14), created for good works (Eph. 2:10), indwelt and empowered by the Holy Spirit (Eph. 1:13–14; Phil. 4:13), endowed with every spiritual blessing (Eph. 1:3), favored with continuous access to the throne of grace (Heb. 4:16), and called to be a partaker of His heavenly calling (Heb. 3:1). Scripture reminds you of who you really are and where your success truly comes from. As Paul writes, "Our adequacy is from God, who also made us adequate as servants of a new covenant" (2 Cor. 3:5–6).

> *Scripture reminds you of who you really are and where your success truly comes from.*

+ **Equipped**—thoroughly furnished to complete every good work. At times, the most difficult thing for any of us to do is finish well. We come to points in our lives when we feel we cannot go on or achieve what we have been given to accomplish. The burdens become too heavy, the decisions too complex, the challenges too disheartening, and the road too bewildering. We wonder if we have what it takes to keep going or if we should just give up. To the follower of Christ, this may be especially confusing when we're just doing what the Savior has called us to do. Why such difficulty and confusion on the path if we have embraced His purposes? But what the Word does in such times is help us complete the journey. It trains us to keep "fixing our eyes on Jesus, the author and perfecter of faith" (Heb. 12:2). Through Scripture, God gives us the spiritual food that fuels us, providing the wisdom and energy we need to keep going each day and confront the obstacles that await us on the path.

So we see that the Word is indeed central to knowing and doing God's will. You cannot truly live the triumphant Christian life apart from it.

But one of the things we must notice here is that Paul writes: "*All Scripture* is inspired by God and profitable" (2 Tim. 3:16, emphasis added). We may wonder at this, especially with some of the amazing and challenging stories we find in the Old Testament. In fact, there are many throughout the ages who have suggested we should minimize or even abandon the Old Testament because of the confusion it can cause to believers and focus only on the New Testament. So our question might be: Did Paul really mean that we should look at *all Scripture* as God breathed and beneficial?

Thankfully, in verse 15 of this same chapter Paul gives us an answer. The apostle Paul wrote to his son in the faith Timothy: "From childhood you have known the sacred writings which are able to give you the wisdom that leads to salvation through faith which is in Christ Jesus." Considering that the majority of—if not all—the New Testament would have been written *after* Timothy was fully grown, the "sacred writings" Paul referred to *had to be* the Old Testament texts. It would have been all the Bible they would have had at the time—with manuscripts compiled by scribes and translated from Hebrew to Greek by scholars around 250 to 100 BC. So the apostle Paul did not merely *include* the Old Testament; he was actually *focused* on it.

In fact, Jesus confirmed the importance of the Old Testament as the foundation of our faith by citing it often as He taught. Luke 24:27 tells us: "Beginning with Moses and with all the prophets, He [Jesus] explained to them the things concerning Himself in all the Scriptures." And as I said before, the Old Testament pointed to Jesus so we would know exactly Who our Messiah would be (John 5:39). Please understand, I am not suggesting that the New Testament is any less important—it beautifully reports and explains the fullness of all Christ has done for us and how He will come again to rule as the King of kings and Lord of lords. Rather, I am affirming that *both* the Old and the New Testaments are extremely important to our relationship with Christ.

Of course, you may wonder, *Why did the Lord make some of His Word so difficult to understand? Why are so many of the things He said so challenging?* I believe the Father did so because if He had made it overly simple, we would not pay it much attention or be interested in taking hold of all its wonderful truths. After all, Proverbs 25:2 says: "It is the glory of God to conceal a matter, but the glory of kings is to search out a matter." There is joy in the discovery. There is fulfillment in digging deep into its context and gleaning its profound meaning. There are verses that we could spend a lifetime studying and still benefit daily from the rich truth they teach us.

> *There are verses that we could spend a lifetime studying and still benefit daily from the rich truth they teach us.*

So as you read Scripture and consider what the Holy Spirit may be communicating to you through it, don't just think, *How do I solve my problem?* Instead, keep the following questions and concepts in mind:

1. Lord, what do You want to communicate to me today? Make those verses and principles stick out and help me to focus on what You desire me to see.

2. What is the context of what I am reading? How do You want me to relate to the testimonies of those in Scripture? Help me to understand the foundation and heart of what has been written.

3. What can I glean about what You desire to accomplish in me and through me?

4. What are You revealing to me about Your character, relationship with me, and provision?

5. Are there attitudes, beliefs, and habits that are undermining my well-being or relationship with You? Are there strongholds You wish to tear down?

6. Father, show me truth with which I can combat those wrongful attitudes, beliefs, habits, and strongholds, and set me on the right path. Bring to mind other passages of Scripture that communicate what You are teaching me.

7. Are there any actions or steps that You are revealing to me through Your Word? How do You desire me to apply what I am reading?

Often we limit His plan to the big choices of life—the great decisions and important crossroad moments. However, His will is accomplished in you step by step— every time you submit to the truth you learn in Scripture and obey the inner promptings of His Holy Spirit.

Friend, your heavenly Father will speak to you. He will bring things to mind He wants to address in your life. No matter what it is, do not push it aside. Instead, continue pursuing how Jesus desires for you to deal with it. Because that, at its most profound core, is doing God's will. Often we limit His plan to the big choices of life—the great decisions and important crossroad moments. However,

His will is accomplished in you step by step—every time you submit to the truth you learn in Scripture and obey the inner promptings of His Holy Spirit.

As I said, the Word of God is an absolute necessity for understanding and living in the will of God. It gives you direction for every area of your life. All of the central issues of your existence are addressed in it. True, it may not speak to particular details of your life such as when to eat, when to check your tires, or what color socks to wear. But you can always make decisions about those details based on the principles of His Word.

Circumstances of Life

A second way God will speak to us is through the circumstances of our lives—through where He puts us, the situations we find ourselves in, and the people He places around us. As we saw previously, the events we experience are not random; rather, they are allowed by God for His good purposes (Rom. 8:28). He is continuously working in our lives on a moment-by-moment basis to direct us in His will and accomplish it through us.

For example, after he had completed his third missionary journey, Paul returned to Jerusalem even though he was warned that to do so meant persecution and imprisonment (Acts 20:22–24, 21:1–14). He had only been in Jerusalem a little more than a week when Jewish leaders incited the crowds against him. Seeing "that all Jerusalem was in confusion" because of Paul's presence, the commander of the Roman cohort there took Paul into custody.

Certainly, being a prisoner had to be disheartening. But Paul kept his focus on Christ. And during his time in Jerusalem, Paul was able to give his testimony to the Roman commander and soldiers who had rescued him, the Jews who had demanded his imprisonment, and the chief priests and

Council of Pharisees and Sadducees (Acts 21:36–23:10). When Paul was moved to Caesarea, he was able to witness first to Governor Felix (Acts 24:10–25), then to his successor Governor Porcius Festus, and also to King Agrippa and Queen Bernice (Acts 25:13–32).

Likewise, when Paul was sent to Rome, he wrote: "I want you to know, brethren, that my circumstances have turned out for the greater progress of the gospel, so that my imprisonment in the cause of Christ has become well known throughout the whole praetorian guard and to everyone else, and that most of the brethren, trusting in the Lord because of my imprisonment, have far more courage to speak the word of God without fear" (Phil. 1:12–14). Who were these men in the praetorian guard? They acted as personal bodyguards for the Roman emperors and their families. They were the elite palace guards, and the Lord, in His providence, found a way to chain them to His most vocal disciple, Paul. In other words, Paul realized that God had given him a congregation that would never have called him to be their pastor—and these guards were a captive audience. They would never have sent him a letter saying: "We would love to know about Jesus; would you please come tell us about Him?" But hear about Jesus they did.

You may be wondering, *What does this have to do with understanding God's will in my circumstances?* What I would like you to see is that there is no way in the world that Paul could have foreseen how God would use him in Rome—how He would work through Paul's arrest in Jerusalem to get him to that point. However, instead of fretting that he was in chains, Paul saw the opportunities in his circumstances. He looked for the possibilities. He remained open to the way God was working in the lives of the men who guarded him.

You may be reading this book completely disheartened that certain relationships and prospects have ended for you. But what you need to see is that the Lord operates through the closed doors just as much as through the open ones. Yes, it can be extremely painful when something you care about ends. During the time of his imprisonment, Paul was no longer able to visit the churches he had planted or the believers he had led to Christ. It was no longer possible for him to evangelize in unreached areas or plant new congregations. The Lord chose to close that

> *The Lord operates through the closed doors just as much as through the open ones.*

door of his ministry, which was excruciating for Paul. However, through that closed door came one that was open to him, which was the ability to reach the praetorian guard. And because of it, not only did Paul write the very powerful prison epistles of Ephesians, Philippians, Colossians, and Philemon, but also the believers in the Roman church—who had been silenced by intense persecution—saw Paul's example and became bold in their witness.

The point is that we may often become discouraged or confused by the choices and blessings God seems to take away from us. However, if we focus only on what we *cannot* do, we often don't realize the opportunities and blessings He has provided for us.

> *If we focus only on what we cannot do, we often don't realize the opportunities and blessings He has provided for us.*

This was certainly true of one of the most difficult trials I have ever experienced, which was when my wife left me. I was absolutely devastated. Not only had my most important earthly relationship fallen apart, but it also caused ripple effects that wreaked havoc on every aspect of my life. I certainly thought that it would destroy my ministry. Who would trust me to teach God's Word now that I was so rejected and wounded? There just wasn't anything I could do about it. I had already tried everything I knew to do and had still failed to prevent the outcome I dreaded most—the loss of my wife.

But to my surprise, this terrible development opened the doors of ministry in a manner I never could have imagined. People began approaching me, saying, "For a long time I couldn't watch your program because I thought you couldn't possibly understand what I felt. I used to think, *What does Dr. Stanley know about all the hurt, pain, and fear I'm facing?* But now I know you appreciate how deeply I am hurting because you've been there, too. And you've helped me a lot." In this manner, God revealed a new and important ministry field to me. He turned the worst heartache of my life into a realization of how others are struggling and how Christ can help them overcome through their times of loneliness and suffering.

The Father can and will do the same in your life if you'll trust Him in all your circumstances—in both your open and closed doors. The details surrounding your life are extremely important, so don't ignore them.

In his devotional book, *My Utmost for His Highest,* Oswald Chambers affirms this, saying: "We can all see God in exceptional things, but it requires the growth of spiritual discipline to see God in every detail. Never believe that the so-called random events of life are anything less than God's appointed order. Be ready to discover His divine designs anywhere and everywhere."

This goes hand in hand with a principle I often teach: ***As children of a sovereign God, we are never victims of our circumstances.*** Our heavenly Father is *always* working through our details, losses, discouragements, obstacles, challenges, problems, opportunities, and victories to direct us on the path of His will.

So take an inventory of your current situation. Has the Father blocked the road before you in either a temporary or permanent manner? Is it because He wants you to stop and wait upon Him or because He no longer wants you to go down that path? What opportunities are available to you? Is there an area where you've suffered that could become an area of ministry to you? Is it possible that the road before you is confusing because God has another path for you altogether?

As I said previously, it will help to spend time in Scripture and in prayer as you consider these questions. Ponder them in your heart, but also allow the Father to speak to you through His Word and during your time before His throne of grace.

Counsel of Godly Christians

Of course, the third, and very important, way God speaks to us is through the godly counsel of other believers. Sometimes we simply need the help of other Christians to know what to do in areas we're unaccustomed to.

This is why Scripture admonishes us to teach one another with love, a good conscience, and a sincere faith (1 Tim. 1:5). Colossians 3:16 instructs: "Let the word of Christ richly dwell within you, with all wisdom teaching and admonishing one another with psalms and hymns and spiritual songs, singing with thankfulness in your hearts to God." The Father understands we sometimes need a human connection and has given us the Body of Christ as a support system for us (Matt. 28:19–20; Rom. 12:6–13; 2 Tim. 2:2, 24).

Therefore, it is both good and wise to turn to godly people when you need help discerning God's will. Proverbs 1:5 says, "A man of understanding will acquire wise counsel." Likewise, Proverbs 19:20 instructs: "Listen to counsel and accept discipline, that you may be wise the rest of your days."

However, the key to this is receiving counsel from those who *honor the Lord.* As Proverbs 13:20 says, "He who walks with wise men will be wise, but the companion of fools will suffer harm." So always consider the people who are influencing you the most. If they are focused on Jesus and love His Word, then they should have a positive impact on your life. However, if you spend your time with ungodly people or listening to advice from secular sources on television or the internet, you will certainly be affected in a negative manner. So you must be very careful.

Do the people you associate with spend time in God's Word? Do they reflect Christ in their lifestyle? Are they wise and loving toward others? Do they have humble spirits that are in submission to the Lord? Do they care about you—about how you are seeking and following Jesus? Do they keep you accountable in the areas where you struggle? Do they keep your concerns confidential? If not, then perhaps it is better to find another source for assistance.

The last person you want to get counsel from is somebody who is actively disobeying the Father. And ultimately, you are responsible for the decisions you make and the actions you take. So you want someone to counsel you who is committed to obeying Him—a Christian who clearly understands how to listen to God and has a strong relationship with Him. Someone who is actively walking in the center of His will, just as you would like to.

Seek out someone to counsel you who is actively walking in the center of His will, just as you would like to.

Of course, no matter how godly or Christ-centered your friends are, never ask them to make your decisions for you. Likewise, do not say, "Would you please tell me God's will for my life?" or, "What should I do?" Most people will have an opinion and would enjoy telling you what to do, but that's not that kind of counsel that is helpful.

You are seeking the Father's will, not just the next step you should take. The process of discovering His plan for your life is about becoming dependent upon Him in your own relationship with Him, not what others say it is.

So instead, ask, "Do you have any insight into what God may be saying to me based on Scripture or how you've seen Him work in your life? What does God's Word say about the decision I am trying to make?"

A godly counselor will be motivated to guide you to the truth—even when it is uncomfortable or it hurts—because he or she will be committed to helping you obediently follow Jesus on His path for your life. So look for people whose desire is for you to have a strong relationship with Christ so you can experience life at its best. Because that's the kind of friend whose counsel you can always trust.

And always—no matter who gives you counsel—confirm what you've heard with the Living God in Scripture and through prayer. Always.

Conscience

A fourth factor in discerning God's will is our conscience, which is the inner voice that acts as a moral filter for us. It is the alarm that goes off within us when we are tempted to do something that isn't right or when we head in the wrong direction. Something within us senses when things are amiss.

Each of us has a conscience, whether we believe in Christ or not. The apostle Paul tells us: "Gentiles, who do not have God's written law, show that they know his law when they instinctively obey it, even without having heard it. They demonstrate that God's law is written in their hearts, for their own conscience and thoughts either accuse them or tell them they are doing right" (Rom. 2:14–15 NLT). So it is a gift we have all been given and we see the conscience can be very helpful as we are seeking the Father's plan and to walk in His will.

However, with this said, I must begin this section with some caveats because we must be extremely careful about listening to our consciences. First, as I said, everyone has a conscience, whether they are saved or not. So there is nothing inherently godly or Christ-centered about the conscience. *Rather, the conscience is going to operate on the basis of how it has been programmed.* Whether or not it is helpful depends a great deal on what media and content you have been consuming—because it all influences your soul, mind, and spirit for good or for bad.

Second, I've seen that people can put a lot of confidence in the internal voice that guides them—more than is warranted. In fact, I've heard people say, "I've always believed in just following my conscience. I let my conscience be my guide." Or they express something more general like, "I just go with my gut," or, "I'm following my heart." But, as I said, this is not always the wisest course of action. And the truth of the matter is that, at times, people have made a complete mess of their lives by obeying it.

For example, how many terrible marriages have begun because people were swept away by their emotions and were wed before it was wise? How many have entered into ruinous business deals because of their gut instincts, which proved catastrophically faulty? How many have followed a path because it "felt right" or "made sense at the time" but found that it led to disaster? This is because the trustworthiness of your conscience is determined by what you feed it and whether or not you truly heed its warnings. After you repeatedly say yes to sin, that alarm within you becomes muffled, more and more difficult to hear.

Finally, what is important to understand is that the purpose of your conscience is not necessarily to *guide you* in decisions—that is not the reason it was given to us. Scripture never counsels believers to follow their consciences alone, because their condition and reliability vary. In fact, the conscience is described in both positive and negative ways throughout the

Bible. The conscience can be "good" (1 Tim. 1:19), "clean" (2 Tim. 1:3), and "blameless" (Acts 24:16). But it can also be "weak" (1 Cor. 8:7–12), "defiled" (Titus 1:15), "evil" (Heb. 10:22), and even "seared," which means it is completely insensitive to sin and unresponsive to the Holy Spirit's promptings (1 Tim. 4:1–2).

Rather, the conscience's main purpose is to protect you or stop you from proceeding on a sinful or dangerous course or to prompt you to do what is right. The unsettling alarm that sounds within us when we're contemplating a disastrous decision is the Father's way of safeguarding us from foolish choices. Likewise, there are times when we know the right thing to do—such as apologize when we have wronged someone or give to someone who is in need. So the conscience gives you feedback but is not necessarily meant to direct you.

> *The conscience's main purpose is to protect you or stop you from proceeding on a sinful or dangerous course or to prompt you to do what is right.*

Sadly, many people want to ignore and even silence this internal warning, so they can "enjoy life" and do whatever they please. They even go so far as picking and choosing what they believe about Christ and what passages of Scripture to submit to—or deny Him and His Word altogether. But when you do so, ignoring the internal warnings, your conscience is no longer reliable and will not accurately guide you. It grows quieter and quieter within you until you are no longer able to hear it altogether. This can be compared to abandoning the helm of a ship during a storm and letting it crash on the rocks. Without that internal navigation, only disaster lies ahead.

Conversely, when we feed the conscience with *wrong* information, such as legalistic religious regulations not found in Scripture, we can fall prey to false guilt. As I have often said, I grew up in a legalistic denomination that had all sorts of rules not found anywhere in Scripture. For example, the leaders of the Pentecostal Holiness church in my town did not approve of any music other than the hymns we would sing on Sundays. Likewise, they thought wearing any kind of jewelry was wrong.

The leaders even considered reading what we used to call the funny papers, or newspaper comic strips, a sin. Well, I delivered newspapers every day as a boy and I remember reading about the excellent detective work of Dick Tracy as he fought crime and the adventures of Little Orphan Annie and her dog, Sandy. I could never understand why anyone would consider such innocent story lines to be sinful. All of their man-made, restrictive rules only served to create false guilt in those who tried to live by them. Thankfully, we don't have to live in this legalistic manner because Christ purchased our freedom on the cross so we could have true liberty in Him (Gal. 5:1).

This is why our greatest protection is found in the unchanging Word of God and the guidance of the Holy Spirit. Whether we receive wrong information from the world or through the church, the Lord can break through the bondage it causes as we seek Him. Scripture and the indwelling Spirit work together with the conscience to steer us in the right direction and prevent us from going wrong.

The truth of the matter is that only a Christ-centered conscience can genuinely protect us. The conscience is reliable only when it is under His lordship. Our internal moral filter becomes more trustworthy when the Word of God is the basis for our conduct, we are motivated by a strong desire to obey the Lord, we prayerfully consider our decisions, and we willingly repent as soon as we are aware of sin in our lives.

If this is true for you, you can trust your conscience because it has been transformed and brought under submission of the Holy Spirit. Whenever you sense its warning, you will know the Lord is giving you clear direction, is helping you to apply scriptural principles to your situation, and will provide the strength to do the right thing. If you've already made a poor choice, He will convict you to change course. The Father is constantly working to protect us as His children, but we must listen to His warnings and allow Him to lead us away from anything that doesn't fit who we are in Christ. Because then we can be certain that we are walking in His will.

So consider: What kind of conscience do you have? Is it one that is sensitive to the Lord and His Word, or do you no longer hear the warnings? Although you may want to rationalize, defend, or excuse your sins, that is a sure recipe for disaster, because no one escapes the consequences of disobedience. God wants us to be truthful, confess our sins, and let Him reprogram us—to make our consciences clean and strong. If they are, we can experience His true peace, joy, and security.

Common Sense

Some people may be surprised to see common sense as the fifth way we can discern God's will, while others may be relieved. The surprise, of course, is because God's ways are so often different from ours. As He tells us in Isaiah 55:8, "'My thoughts are not your thoughts, nor are your ways My ways,' declares the LORD." We expect God's will to be beyond us and even contrary to our common sense.

For example, when Abraham was seventy-five years old the Lord told him he would have a son through whom the entire world would be blessed. Then God had Abraham wait an additional twenty-five years. Common sense would tell you that this was an impossible promise for the Lord to fulfill or for Abraham to believe in. Yet this departure from common sense was for the purpose of testing Abraham's faith. And Romans 4:19–20 testifies that Abraham passed the test: "Without becoming weak in faith he [Abraham] contemplated his own body, now as good as dead since he was about a hundred years old, and the deadness of Sarah's womb; yet, with respect to the promise of God, he did not waver in unbelief but grew strong in faith, giving glory to God." We see story after story like this in Scripture.

However, what we must realize is that not every decision is outside of what the Father has already revealed to us. For example, it is wise to eat a healthy diet, get proper rest, and exercise. Conversely, it is foolish to smoke, drink, or do drugs because of the possibility of addiction and the side effects so often associated with these behaviors.

But the way God can work through common sense goes much deeper than this. Perhaps you recall the story of Samson, who was a mighty judge in Israel before the nation had kings. At the time, Israel was being oppressed by a people known as the Philistines and the Lord raised up Samson to free the Jewish people from their terrible grasp. The way God empowered Samson to do so was through supernaturally great strength. In fact, we are told that with the "fresh jawbone of a donkey . . . he [Samson] . . . killed a thousand [Philistine] men" (Judg. 15:15). So, as you may imagine, the Philistines were anxious to get rid of him.

If you recall, Samson eventually fell in love with a woman named Delilah, who lived in the Valley of Sorek and was allied with the Philistines. Judges 16:6 reports: "Delilah said to Samson, 'Please tell me where your great strength is and how you may be bound to afflict you.'" Now, it is normal for couples to share their most intimate details with each other. However, considering that this was not just a personal secret, but one that was central to the security and welfare of Israel, one wouldn't blame Samson for keeping the true source of his strength concealed.

But instead of Samson telling Delilah that he could not disclose his secret, he says that binding him with seven fresh cords would weaken him. He lies to her, which is a red flag in itself—showing that not only does he not trust her, but also his view of their relationship is inherently damaged. If you ever feel you must respond to someone or something in a sinful manner—such as being deceitful— then there is something fundamentally wrong with the situation itself or your motives in it.

If you ever feel you must respond to someone or something in a sinful manner—such as being deceitful—then there is something fundamentally wrong with the situation itself or your motives in it.

Of course, we know there was something terribly wrong with Samson and Delilah's relationship and that he was right not to tell her. As one might expect, while he was asleep Delilah tied Samson with seven fresh cords and called out, "The Philistines are upon you, Samson!" while Philistine soldiers waited in the next room (vv. 7–9).

His unbound body, obviously, was not the true source of Samson's strength. But at this point, common sense should have raised an alarm for Samson. Or at least, it should have when Delilah did the same thing a second time. Delilah asked how to bind Samson and he replied, "Bind me tightly with new ropes which have not been used" (v. 10). He deceives her again. So she waited until he was asleep, bound him with new ropes, and again called out, "The Philistines are upon you, Samson!" while Philistine soldiers waited in the next room (v. 12).

Delilah did this again a third time as well—repeating the same pattern.

Finally, Judges 16:16 tells us, "It came about when she pressed him daily with her words and urged him, that his soul was annoyed to death."

At this point, Samson's common sense should have kicked into overdrive, steering him clear of Delilah altogether. She was neither treating him with respect nor being loving toward him. Instead, she was nagging him—focused on wearing him down in order to discover what would destroy him, so the Philistines could subjugate Israel.

But instead of fleeing from Delilah, which would have been the wise course of action, Samson made a disastrous decision. He foolishly gave in and told her his secret: "A razor has never come on my head, for I have been a Nazirite to God from my mother's womb. If I am shaved, then my strength will leave me and I will become weak and be like any other man" (v. 17). As one may suspect, this was the beginning of the end for Samson. The Philistines were finally able to capture and subdue their great Israelite opponent (vv. 18–21).

We may think of Samson's story as an extraordinary tale that doesn't have much to do with how we live and operate. However, it shows us that God can and does reveal areas of our life that are not serving us well. Samson had warning after warning about what Delilah was after, but he ignored them. In the same way, we may take a course of action and fail. We try it again and fail again. We do the same thing over and over and wonder why it never works out for us. In such instances, the Father endeavors to work through our common sense to show us the areas in which we are not operating in His will—to show us that what we are doing is defeating us rather than leading us to success.

For example, when I was a boy we didn't have much money at all. But I remember seeing a sale of ten pairs of socks for a dollar. I thought I'd struck gold. I bought two dollars' worth of socks—twenty pairs in all—and went home thinking I had uncovered a great secret of commerce: If I buy things cheaply, I can buy a lot more.

Do you know how long those socks lasted? By the second time I wore them, they started unraveling all over the place. Common sense taught me that a bargain isn't always worthwhile—sometimes it is a trap. Sometimes it just means poorer quality that will fall apart a whole lot more quickly.

Now, that is just a simple illustration, but what God can reveal to us through our common sense can be quite serious. For instance, people may drink to escape their problems—only to find they feel worse the next day and their troubles are still there. Or perhaps people will try to buy their way to a sense of worth, freedom, and acceptability. But they discover that what they've purchased for themselves actually makes them feel more emptiness, bondage, and loneliness.

This was certainly true for Samson. He was trying to fulfill his needs for love, companionship, and sexual intimacy through Delilah, who was out to destroy him. So in order to keep Delilah, he lied to her. That never makes for a healthy, fulfilling relationship. The way they related to each other was destructive to its core.

So common sense aids us by leading us to the point of realization that we are trying to achieve our goals in the wrong way. The Spirit-controlled believer is to use his or her head when discerning the will of God.

> *Common sense aids us by leading us to the point of realization that we are trying to achieve our goals in the wrong way.*

Titus 2:11–12 affirms this, saying, "The grace of God has appeared, bringing salvation to all men, instructing us to deny ungodliness and worldly desires and to live sensibly"—or using common sense—"righteously and godly in the present age." In other words, instead of pursuing our deep inner needs in our worldly and ineffective ways—which just don't work (Prov. 16:25)—we choose Jesus' way—which is always right, good, and true. We are guided by the Holy Spirit, Who knows the best way to supply *all* our needs (Phil. 4:19).

So consider: Are there areas of your life that are not working the way you thought they would? Are you attempting to deaden areas of pain with illicit substances, destructive activities, or relationships that are actually deepening your sense of emptiness, pain, and isolation? Are you trying to hold on to some situation, thing, or person that is leading you down a dark road—causing you to move further and further away from God and His purposes for your life?

If something is not working in a godly, productive manner, be honest with yourself and admit it. Then seek the Lord through His Word and in prayer to learn how to turn your situation around.

Compulsion

A sixth way we learn God's will is through compulsion, which I spoke about briefly in the previous chapter when discussing how the Father communicates with you on a daily basis. These are the ways that the Spirit of God speaks to your heart and prompts you to act. This is a principle that we have seen in Philippians 2:13: "It is God who is at work in you, both to will and to work for His good pleasure." The Lord gives you the strong desire or the impulse to do His will.

This can happen in any number of ways, but I will give you a simple example from my own life. Not long ago, I woke up at around 1:30 on a Saturday morning, feeling miserable—my nose was completely stopped up and I couldn't breathe. I got up, walked around, and prayed, "Lord, tomorrow's Sunday and I have to preach. I'm not going to make it feeling like this. Please show me what to do."

The next thing I knew, I had a strong urge to have some chicken soup. I couldn't get away from this impulse to have some. So I went and looked in my cabinets and pantry. All I had was some tomato sauce and a can of black-eyed peas. No chicken soup. I thought, *Well, nobody ever got healed eating black-eyed peas.*

It was like God said, "Where do you find chicken soup?"

I couldn't imagine the Lord wanted me to go to the grocery store at 1:30 in the morning. But I could feel Him speaking to my heart, "Tomorrow is Sunday. You don't want to miss it and I don't want you to miss it. I intend for you to be there. Go get you some chicken soup."

So I did. I got dressed, went down to the store, bought three cans of chicken soup, and cooked it. Almost as soon as I started eating, I began to feel better. I rested and prayed all day that Saturday and I felt fine preaching the next day.

When you sense God is moving you in a particular direction or to do something, don't try to reason it out. Just do what He tells you to do. Of course, it is always important to test where the impulses are coming from (1 John 4:1). If they are sinful, you know they aren't coming from the Holy Spirit.

Galatians 5:16 instructs: "Walk by the Spirit, and you will not carry out the desire of the flesh." The flesh is our tendency to rebel against God's will for our lives. But what does it mean to "walk by the Spirit"? This signifies that we live each moment in dependence on the Holy Spirit, sensitive to His voice, and obedient to His promptings. As we go throughout each day, we are listening for the Father to speak to us and when He does we obey. For example, we may be convicted to flee from something that is tempting us to sin, we may be compelled to contact and encourage someone who is hurting, or we may feel led to do something unusually kind for a stranger. These are all ways God compels us to act in His will.

Now, I have given you minor illustrations of how the Spirit works to urge us to action. But He often speaks in much more important aspects of our lives as well. For example, I've often had young people come to me and say that they feel like the Father has called them into the ministry. Then they will ask, "How can I know for sure whether God is calling me to serve Him?" Of course, this is always music to my ears as a pastor, and there are several things I would tell them—such as the need to identify their spiritual gifts and serve Him right where they are while they discern His will.

However, some of the most important and telling evidence that you are supposed to serve God is that deep down inside of you there's this awesome sense of compulsion. You feel compelled to give your life to Jesus and can't imagine doing anything else. As the apostle Paul wrote, "The love of Christ compels us . . . He died for all, that those who live should live no longer for themselves, but for Him who died for them and rose again" (2 Cor. 5:14–15 NKJV). Because of all Jesus has given for you, you cannot conceive of doing anything else but living for Him.

> *"The love of Christ compels us . . . He died for all, that those who live should live no longer for themselves, but for Him who died for them and rose again."*
> —2 Corinthians 5:14–15 NKJV

So if you are asking the Father if He's called you to preach the gospel or serve Him in some way, consider whether anything else is even an option for you. Certainly, you may have gifts in other areas. But if you find that your internal drive is set on serving Him and making the name of Jesus known to others, then yes, God is calling you.

But I would like to stop here and address something important. I speak with many people who desire to serve Christ, but they are doubtful of their call because they feel inadequate, sinful, and unworthy of representing the name of Jesus. In fact, I have found that it is when people truly want to dedicate their lives to Him that they go through some of the deepest times of brokenness and self-condemnation of their lives. They are horribly aware of every fault, sin, and errant thought—even to the point of being completely debilitated by them. They wonder if this deepened sense of their own wickedness is God's way of rejecting them.

Friend, take heart. The closer we get to God, the more we are aware of our mistakes and failings. We see this in the life of Isaiah, the great prophet who faithfully served the Lord and the nations of Israel and Judah throughout the eighth century BC.

Isaiah wrote: "In the year of King Uzziah's death I saw the Lord sitting on a throne, lofty and exalted, with the train of His robe filling the temple. Seraphim stood above Him . . . and one called out to another and said, 'Holy, Holy, Holy, is the LORD of hosts, the whole earth is full of His glory'" (Isa. 6:1–3). Of course, seeing the Living God in all His glory would be a very humbling and overwhelming experience indeed. But take note of Isaiah's spontaneous response: "Woe is me, for I am ruined! Because I am a man of unclean lips, and I live among a people of unclean lips; for my eyes have seen the King, the LORD of hosts" (v. 5). Immediately, when confronted with God's perfect holiness, Isaiah is overwhelmed with his own sense of falling short.

This is what happens when you get closer to God. Your understanding of your sinfulness increases—not because He is rejecting you, but because He is holy. But realize that God does not reveal your faults in order to condemn you. Rather, He does so in order to heal you, forgive you, and cleanse you from all that keeps you bound (1 John 1:9).

Look at what happened to Isaiah: "Then one of the seraphim flew to me with a burning coal in his hand . . . he touched my mouth with it and said, 'Behold, this has touched your lips; and your iniquity is taken away and your sin is forgiven'" (vv. 6–7). Isaiah became aware of his sin, and God immediately sent provision to free him from it.

The same is true for you. Your heavenly Father doesn't desire for you to remain in the attitudes, behaviors, and strongholds that are destroying you. He wants to set you free so you can become all that you were created to be.

> *Your heavenly Father wants to set you free so you can become all that you were created to be.*

We know this because of the very next thing that happens to Isaiah: "Then I [Isaiah] heard the voice of the Lord, saying, 'Whom shall I send, and who will go for Us?' Then I said, 'Here am I. Send me!'" Do you see that? God didn't allow Isaiah to feel broken in order to reject him. He permitted it so Isaiah could be prepared for his mission.

Again, this same process is at work in your life. You may be feeling your deep and seemingly pervasive sinfulness to a point of despair just like Isaiah did. But also, like Isaiah, all of your self-centeredness and self-sufficiency must burn off so you can become useful to the One you desire to serve. Because ultimately, ministry is exalting Christ, not ourselves. Remember what Jesus said: "I, if I am lifted up from the earth, will draw all men to Myself" (John 12:32). So if this is what you are feeling, do not despair. As I have often said, *brokenness is God's requirement for maximum usefulness.* The process is difficult, but I can testify that it is completely worthwhile.

Contentment

A seventh way we are given to discern God's will is through the contentment or tranquility we feel when proceeding on a course of action. Perhaps you have heard people say, "I just don't have any peace about it," when speaking about a particular decision. The principle here is that when you are either outside the Lord's will or working *against* Him, you will feel spiritual friction that makes you uncomfortable. But when you are in the center of God's will, you will feel harmony with Him—a peace "which surpasses all comprehension," so to speak (Phil. 4:7).

Most of us can point to areas of our lives that cause stress, unhappiness, and turmoil. Some things we can change; many we cannot. But regardless of the situation, any believer can find tranquility in Christ. Jesus told His disciples, "My peace I give to you; not as the world gives do I give to you. Do not let your heart be troubled, nor let it be fearful" (John 14:27). He is the One Who can be our assurance and security regardless of our circumstances. When bad times come, we can put our focus on Him rather than the source of stress—realizing the great Defender we have in the loving Savior who never lets us down. Through understanding Who He is, we can have contentment in the midst of pain, heartache, suffering, and misfortune, because He never leaves us or forsakes us (Deut. 31: 6, 8).

But more specifically, the supernatural peace Jesus promises us rests on our agreement with Him. This is why Colossians 3:15 tells us, "Let the peace of Christ rule in your hearts." When you submit your daily choices to Him, you not only are in harmony with His Holy Spirit, but you also are safeguarded within His protection, enlightened with His wisdom, and empowered by His strength. This is a choice we make. However, the peace we experience can also be evidence to us that we are, indeed, walking in His will.

For example, perhaps you have a decision before you with five good choices. As time goes on, different factors arise reducing that number of options down to two very good ones. With one, you have peace; with the other, you don't. Friend, do not be mistaken; the Lord is speaking to you. When you have searched the Word, prayed, examined your choices clearly, and have that deep sense of abiding tranquility, you can know for certain that's the step God is moving you to take.

It doesn't have to make sense. In fact, sometimes what the Lord leads you to do will appear unreasonable, which I will talk about later. But when you are walking in the center of God's will, you will feel His tranquility, even if everything around you is chaotic. And you are promised that "the peace of God, which surpasses all comprehension, will guard your hearts and your minds in Christ Jesus" (Phil. 1:7).

Communication with God Through Prayer

This brings us to the eighth and final way God communicates His plans to us, which is through prayer. Throughout this chapter, I have been talking about all the ways God reveals His will: through the circumstances of life, the counsel of godly Christians, your conscience, common sense, compulsion, and contentment. And as I said at the beginning of this chapter, all of these factors must be measured against God's Word, because He would never tell us anything that contradicts what He has written in Scripture. So we began with the Bible because it is the best way to learn His voice, how He responds, and what He expects.

However, I also said that we must also communicate with God through prayer, so that He can make sense of what we are experiencing and understand how He desires for us to proceed. As I expressed earlier, the Father reveals the meaning of all the other points—circumstances, counsel, conscience, common sense, compulsion, and contentment— through these two practices. The Lord will work through your time in *communion* and *communication* with Him—through His Word and in prayer—to show how everything works together to reveal His plan for your life.

But how are we to pray for God's will? Many times, when you and I come before the Father in prayer we are in the dark. We don't even know what to ask for or how to approach Him with the questions in our hearts. But remember, God *wants* to communicate His will to you. This is why James 1:5 instructs: "If any of you lacks wisdom, let him ask of God, who gives to all generously and without reproach, and it will be given to him." The Father's desire is to interact and communicate with you.

In fact, this is the very reason He gives you His Holy Spirit. Romans 8:26–27 affirms, "The Spirit also helps our weakness; for we do not know how to pray as we should, but the Spirit Himself intercedes for *us* with groanings too deep for words; and He who searches the hearts knows what the mind of the Spirit is, because He intercedes for the saints according to the will of God."

Did you see that? When you don't know what to pray, the Holy Spirit does so for you, *according to the Lord's will.* He intercedes for you in full agreement with the very purposes for which God created you.

> *The Holy Spirit intercedes for you in full agreement with the very purposes for which God created you.*

Likewise, remember who the Holy Spirit is. He is described in Isaiah 11:2 as "the Spirit of the LORD . . . the spirit of wisdom and understanding, the spirit of counsel and strength, the spirit of knowledge and the fear of the LORD."

✦ First, He is the ***Spirit of the Lord***, which means that everything He does will be consistent with God's plans and character. The Holy Spirit is a member of the Godhead, the third Person of the Trinity. He is God Himself. So everything He does is the Lord's will.

+ He is the ***Spirit of wisdom***—He helps us to live out what is right in the Father's sight and conforms us to the image of Christ.

+ He is the ***Spirit of understanding***—He gives us supernatural discernment into our circumstances, allowing His fruit—"love, joy, peace, patience, kindness, goodness, faithfulness, gentleness, self-control" (Gal. 5:22–23)—to flow through us.

+ He is the ***Spirit of counsel***—He advises us, showing us what to do in every situation and bringing to remembrance everything Christ taught us (John 14:26).

+ He is the ***Spirit of strength***—which means might and valor to do mighty deeds. In other words, the Holy Spirit enables, empowers, and equips us to do God's will—in both endurance and giftedness.

+ He is the ***Spirit of knowledge***—He provides the inventiveness and resourcefulness for the tasks He directs us to accomplish. The Holy Spirit endows us with expert skill for our calling.

+ And He is ***the Spirit of the fear of the Lord***—He teaches us how to honor, respect, and obey the Father.

So the first thing you should know when you are praying to God is that ***you have exactly what you need to interact with Him—you have the Holy Spirit communicating to you and for you.***

But the second point is that ***Jesus leads you to do His will in a very***

special and powerful way in prayer. Remember what we are taught in
Hebrews 4:14–16:

> Therefore, since we have a great high priest who has passed through
> the heavens, Jesus the Son of God, let us hold fast our confession.
> For we do not have a high priest who cannot sympathize with our
> weaknesses, but One who has been tempted in all things as *we are,*
> *yet* without sin. Therefore let us draw near with confidence to the
> throne of grace, so that we may receive mercy and find grace to
> help in time of need.

Jesus is described as our Great High Priest. We know that in the Old
Testament the high priests were the supreme religious leaders over the
priesthood and the people. They were responsible for leading the Israelites
to know and do God's will. Likewise, they represented the people as they
made sacrifices at the temple.

But whereas Old Testament high priests were often separated from the
people because of Levitical laws, their service at the temple, and other reasons, we don't have that problem with Jesus. When Hebrews 4:14 says "we
have a great high priest," the word *have* indicates in an emphatic manner
that Jesus is *continually* available to us. Our Savior is always ready, willing,
and able to receive us to discuss whatever may be on our hearts.

Likewise, Jesus "has passed through the heavens" (v. 14). He knows
what heaven—or our eternal home in glory—is like and what it will require
of us. He has seen what the entire universe looks like from the throne of
God and realizes what we need to do to be prepared for everlasting life
there with Him.

But Christ has also lived on earth and is intimately acquainted with
what we face here as well. Verse 15 says, "We do not have a high priest who

cannot sympathize with our weaknesses, but One who has been tempted in all things as we are, yet without sin." As our Great High Priest, Jesus has compassion for us. During His time on earth, He suffered hunger, thirst, weariness, betrayal, and all the human emotions you and I do.

Hebrews 2:17–18 tells us the reason: "He had to be made like His brethren in all things, so that He might become a merciful and faithful high priest in things pertaining to God, to make propitiation for the sins of the people. For since He Himself was tempted in that which He has suffered, He is able to come to the aid of those who are tempted." Notice that Jesus shared in our humanity and was made like us so He could be *merciful* and *faithful* to us. So He could truly grasp how to help us when we are tempted to sin.

> *Jesus shared in your humanity and was made like you so He could be* merciful *and* faithful *to you. So He could truly grasp how to help you when you are tempted.*

Friend, Jesus sympathizes with you and understands what it is like to be you. Let that incredible thought sink in. You may feel like no one in the world understands you—your deepest questions, your aspirations, and your most profound hurts. But Jesus does. He's experienced everything that you have—rejection, ridicule, and even hardships within His earthly family. And He has compassion for you.

But realize that Jesus knows not only *why* you do what you do but also *what it will take* to help you walk in His will. As the One Who "has been tempted in all things as we are, yet without sin" (Heb. 4:15), your Savior is well aware of the tactics the enemy will try to use to get you to step off God's path and sin. He comprehends why you may cling to unhealthy habits in order to protect yourself. And He has the very best plan—one informed by both heaven and earth—for freeing you and teaching you to walk in His will.

So Hebrews 4:16 admonishes, "Therefore let us draw near with confidence to the throne of grace, so that we may receive mercy and find grace to help in time of need." Have you ever truly considered the seat of power you have been invited to approach? This is not an earthly chair that can be tarnished or destroyed. Nor is it one that can ever be overthrown—its Sovereign King is permanent, all-powerful, and everlasting. You have been invited to come near the throne of the Living God.

Revelation 4 tells us:

Behold, a throne was standing in heaven, and One sitting on the throne. And He who was sitting was like a jasper stone and a sardius in appearance; and there was a rainbow around the throne, like an emerald in appearance.... Out from the throne come flashes of lightning and sounds and peals of thunder. And there were seven lamps of fire burning before the throne, which are the seven Spirits of God; and before the throne there was something like a sea of glass, like crystal; and in the center and around the throne, four living creatures (vv. 2–3, 5–6).

The picture we are given is beyond comprehension—with light emanating from the throne in an array of colors so vibrantly spectacular that the apostle John compares them to jewels. This is not a quiet or sleepy place. No, lightning and peals of thunder surround the throne and there are unimaginable attendants worshiping and serving the Living God with songs of praise.

But on the throne of grace is the One you long to see. It is the immortal, invincible, all-powerful, all-knowing God—the Sovereign of heaven, earth, and all creation. The entire universe is spread out before Him in its great and majestic expanse. But He also sees the room where you kneel to pray and the people you are interceding for in the smallest detail, including the hairs He has numbered on your head. He is so near to you and to them that He can catch your tears, hear your whispers, and touch your hearts.

And even as you don't know how to pray before your great and eternal God, the Holy Spirit is praying through you. He has searched out the deepest groans of your inner self—the most profound needs and wounds there—and He is translating them according to the Father's will.

Likewise, Hebrews 7:25 tells you Jesus "always lives to make intercession" for you. And friend, your Savior does not pray powerlessly. He does not intercede as we often do—hesitantly and bound by limitations. No, your Redeemer prays with authority and unmeasurable capability! This is the voice of the Great I Am—omnipotent in power and omniscient in wisdom.

This is the same voice that called the heaven and the earth into existence. "When He spoke, the world began! It appeared at his command" (Ps. 33:9 NLT). God said, "Let there be light," and light was created (Gen. 1:3). He declared the onset of time and the seconds, minutes, hours, days, months, and years started their count. He spoke and the sun, moon, stars, planets, and every other celestial body were formed and set on their galactic courses. "The

> *The same voice that called the heaven and the earth into existence— that upholds and maintains and propels all things—is the voice that intercedes for you.*

Son is . . . upholding and maintaining and propelling all things [the entire physical and spiritual universe] by His powerful word" (Heb. 1:3 AMP).

That is Jesus. That, friend, is the voice that intercedes *for you*.

Christ is continuously deploying His resources on your behalf. He is the One Who speaks through the Scripture you read, the circumstances of your life, the counsel of godly Christians, your conscience, common sense, compulsion, and can give you that feeling of contentment when you walk in His will. He orchestrates everything you need—moving people, resources, situations, and even changing you—all to carry out His wonderful will for your life. Even the struggles you are experiencing today He is communicating through—engineering the details, limits, and solutions that concern you—all to prepare you, draw you closer to Himself, and teach you to walk in His purposes for your life.

So you don't have to be afraid about missing God's will or misinterpreting what He is trying to say. You also don't have to worry about accomplishing His plan once He reveals it to you. The Lord God is able to speak to you clearly and empower you to do whatever He calls you to do.

However, you do have to *listen* to Him.

In your times of prayer, it is necessary to stop talking long enough to hear what Jesus has to say to you. Then, once you do, you must actively apply what He's said to your life.

Therefore, keep each of the points I showed you in the forefront of your thinking as you make decisions each day. On a three-by-five card write:

Communion with God through Scripture

Circumstances of Life

Counsel of Godly Christians

Conscience

Common Sense

Compulsion

Contentment

Communication with God through Prayer

Think about these things. Spend time in God's Word. Bathe everything in prayer—time before the throne of grace where you *listen* to the Father.

Because God *will* show you His plan when you seek Him and set your heart to hear what He is saying to you.

5

THE HINDRANCES

What's Stopping Your Progress

Naturally, after reading the last chapter you should feel great confidence about knowing and doing the will of God. After all, the One Who spoke the world into existence is the same One speaking to you. If He can set the sun, moon, stars, and galaxies in their places, the Lord certainly can and will communicate His desires to you.

So why is it that sometimes you just don't hear Him? You know that a godly parent would never cease to speak to his or her child—to teach a son or daughter, guide the child to grow in faith and maturity, and help that youngster find the best path for his or her life. In the same way, your heavenly Father will never stop speaking, instructing, and directing you. In fact, Matthew 7:11 promises, "If you then, being evil, know how to give good gifts to your children, how much more will your Father who is in heaven give what is good to those who ask Him!" So if you are experiencing a lack of communication with the Lord, it is not because God is unable or unwilling to connect with you.

Friend, there are times when the problem of hearing the Father lies with us. Now, that doesn't mean He is unable get through to you. As I said in chapter 2, He can and will break through to you if you desire to hear Him. What He will not do is *force* Himself on you—He will not override your refusal to hear Him.

So what are the issues and attitudes that may unwittingly be obstructing your relationship with Jesus and hindering you from knowing His will? In this chapter, we will consider several factors that can block your ability to hear Him. These issues become like noise in your life that stops you from being able to discern what the Lord is saying to you. He is speaking, but because of the clamor for your attention, it is difficult for you to ascertain what He is communicating to you.

Self-Will

Of course, the most common and destructive of these factors is our own self-will. We are so focused on our own needs and desires that we cannot hear what the Lord is telling us.

For example, there may be a driving goal in your life. Perhaps it is to make your business grow, attain a certain level of status in life, or have a certain kind of relationship, like getting married or becoming a parent. You know what it is because it consumes your thoughts, your prayers, and your sleepless nights. That is what you are centered on. Solving the issues surrounding that one objective are always in the forefront of your thinking and it is very difficult for you to consider much else. Sadly, that laser-like focus can at times blind you to other important aspects of your life, including God's will.

I recall sitting on the front porch of a man who was set on asking a young woman to marry him. The driving goal of his life was to have a wife and family. But I had watched him interact with his intended fiancée and could see that their relationship was destructive—they were constantly arguing, manipulating each other, and in competition for who would make the decisions. I did my best to counsel him. I urged him to seek God, discussed how their personalities were incompatible, and explained how a marriage would be difficult to maintain with such differences and obstacles.

I will never forget what he told me. He responded, "I hear what you're saying, but I'm going to do it anyway. I think having a solid commitment will bring us the stability we need to make our relationship work."

Their marriage lasted six weeks.

So completely set on being married, they ignored all the warning signs—including the fact that they made each other miserable. Now, after such a devastating mistake, one may have thought that fellow would have learned a lesson. That he would have received counsel about his relationships and been more careful. But he did the same thing again—a few times. He continued to rush into commitments that were destructive.

When we desire something to fill our inner needs in such an intense manner, we can be blinded by our desires to the point that we do not pay attention to anything else. At the core of this driving impulse is our self-will. Self is that uncontrolled impulse inside of us that demands its own way.

So when considering the pursuit of God's will, we must be aware that our minds may be so full of thoughts about our particular goals that we become insensitive to the Lord's warnings about them. We may also become deaf to all of the other issues the Father is attempting to address in our lives—the ones that are suffering because of our singular focus. How often have businessmen and -women been so focused on success at work that their families have fallen apart? How often have talented believers failed to pursue the great gifts God has given them because they've been so intent on chasing relationships that never fulfill the true yearnings of their hearts? We may be so focused on our driving goal that we fail to hear His direction and guidance about other equally important aspects of our lives.

Does that mean the Lord is unwilling to meet those deep desires of your heart? Of course not. Yes, He may have other objectives for you to accomplish. But He is not insensitive to the longings in you. However, He is also vigilant to ensure that nothing else takes residence on the throne of your heart—which is His rightful place and His alone.

> *God is sensitive to the longings in you. However, He is also vigilant to ensure that nothing else takes residence on the throne of your heart— which is His rightful place alone.*

You see, this is part of our fallen nature—the self wants to control and dominate, pursuing its own goals regardless of what is good or even best for us and others. Our flesh fights against God's Spirit for rulership of our lives, driven by the desire to protect ourselves and soothe the profound hungers within us. With our minds we may acknowledge, "Yes, the Lord knows what is best," but we continue to strive for independence and self-determination. Sadly, the biggest problems we face are usually in the same areas we insist on controlling—unaware that our efforts are actually making things worse rather than better.

For example, that man I just mentioned, who kept marrying the wrong women, had a profound need to feel respected. When he was growing up, he was belittled and made to feel like nothing by domineering and angry parents. So in an effort to fill that vacuum within him, he unconsciously looked for women who shared his parents' traits—who were controlling and condescending—in an effort to "win them over," change their minds, and find the respect he so yearned for. You can immediately see the difficulty in what he was attempting to achieve. He continually looked to fill his needs in all the wrong places, set himself up for failure, and rewounded himself over and over again.

This is what happens in us when we allow areas of self-will to rule. Those are the parts of us that have the most bondage from the defenses and coping mechanisms we have built up throughout our lives; and, therefore, they become the most difficult to surrender to God. We are afraid to lose control. We fear our needs will not be met, our desires will not be fulfilled, or we will miss out on the most important experiences that life has to offer.

But what you and I must ask is: "Would God deny me anything that is truly good for me? Would Jesus—the Savior Who gave His life on the cross so that I can live—really say no to something that would truly bless me, build me up, or strengthen me?" I hope you realize the answer is, "Of course not." If God says, "Wait," or, "No," to something you have been praying for it is because He has a good reason for it.

> *If God says, "Wait," or, "No," to something you have been praying for it is because He has a good reason for it.*

Romans 8:32 reminds us, "He who did not spare His own Son, but delivered Him over for us all, how will He not also with Him freely give us all things?" God wants to plant true, unshakable contentment, peace, security, and joy in your life.

But perhaps you are thinking, *Dr. Stanley, you don't know the incredible losses I've had in my life—the people and things God has allowed to be taken from me. I have to protect myself.*

Friend, I understand the excruciating pain of losing what's important.

I have had numerous seasons of intense brokenness, betrayal, loneliness, and defeat. And I can testify that even though those were the most difficult times of my life, they were also the most fruitful. It was in those times that the Father shook me free from bondage that I had no idea was even in me.

In fact, that is one of the main reasons the Lord allows people to go through great trials and seasons of brokenness—He is trying to liberate them of their self-will so they can recognize the hurt they cause themselves and their unhealthy dependencies on people and possessions that cannot last.

God has identified what must be healed if you are going to become what He has created you to be and reach your full, wonderful, most meaningful, soul-satisfying potential.

If your Savior is in the process of working in some area of your life, He knows what it will take in order for that deep longing within you to truly be filled. He's identified what must be healed if you are going to become what He has created you to be and reach your full, wonderful, most meaningful, soul-satisfying potential.

So surrender your mind, will, emotion, body, soul, and spirit to our heavenly Father, saying, "Lord, I submit to Your will and Your rule in my life. I yield to Your plans and Your methods of accomplishing them. I realize that at times what You desire for me will be different from the longings I have in my own heart. So please identify the areas where I am driven to the point of missing Your plan. I also acknowledge that You know what is best for me and if I delight myself in You, You will fulfill the most profound desires, hopes, and dreams within me. Thank You that I can always trust You. Amen."

Influence of Others

The second factor that can hinder us from knowing God's will is the influence of other people. In the last chapter, I explained that the Father can speak to us powerfully through *godly* counsel. But I also said that we must be very careful about who it is that's guiding us because we can miss the Lord's plan if we're listening to the wrong voices. Because our friends and loved ones can be very sincere in being there for us and wanting to help us know what to do. However, they can also be sincerely wrong.

I can still remember the day when the Lord drove this principle home in my heart. I was sixteen and was meeting a group of buddies at the local drugstore, which was about a mile away from where I lived. Our usual practice was to visit there, have some chocolate shakes, and discuss what we would do for the rest of the evening.

My friends were good fellows who loved God. We never got into or caused trouble, so I had no reason to think they would ever lead me in the wrong direction. But in the course of the conversation, one of them suggested going over and checking out the local pool hall and playing a game. Unfortunately, in those days pool halls were known primarily for their drinking and gambling. They were really nothing more than beer joints. Of course, my buddies swore that they wouldn't have any alcohol and assured me that no one would ever know that we'd been there. But instantly I knew that my friends were going down a bad path. Would I go with the guys in order to maintain the friendships that had always been so important to me? I realized that on the one hand, if I didn't go with them things might never be the same between me and those friends. That was a painful reality. But on the other hand, there was my relationship with God and my calling to consider. I could not deny that the Holy Spirit was speaking clearly to my heart, "Don't go. Don't do that."

I'm sure I hesitated for a moment, because I cared for my friends deeply. I knew that they would never intentionally do anything to harm me or my relationship with Christ. They were merely curious about the pool hall and most likely just wanted to have some innocent fun. But in my heart, I knew that it wasn't for me. I didn't know how going there might hurt my testimony or send me down a destructive path, but I didn't want to find out. If the Father was telling me not to go, there was a good reason for it even if I could not see it or understand it at the moment. So I said, "No, I'm not going to do that. I'm going home." And I walked away.

I won't say it was easy, because it wasn't—not by a long shot. I struggled terribly with loneliness at that moment, fearful I had lost my friends. But I know I did what was right. As I walked up that dark street by myself, the Father said to me clearly, "You will never regret this decision." And the truth of the matter is, I never have. I know that by submitting to the Lord in that instance I took an important step forward in walking in His will for my life instead of being driven by the pressures and beliefs of others.

People have influence in our lives and they will always have an opinion when we have a decision to make. The problem is that they are not you and probably know even less of what God's will is for your life than you do. They sift what they see as your choice through their own personality, needs, values, and perspective. So you cannot rely upon other people to discover the Lord's plan for you. Can you call on godly friends for wise counsel about what the Bible says concerning your situation? As I just said, yes, you can. But as I also said in the previous chapter you must be very wise about who

You cannot rely upon other people to discover the Lord's plan for you.

you allow to speak into your life. The ungodly influence of others can lead you to wrong decisions and even *away* from the Lord's path for you. So when there are forks in the road and you don't know what to do, you cannot take a public vote among your friends or family members concerning your course of action. You have to listen to God.

Take King Rehoboam for example. In 1 Kings 12, we find that Rehoboam needed wise counsel about how to rule Israel. Shortly after he became king, the people of Israel came and asked that he lighten the heavy yoke that his father, Solomon, had placed on them through high taxation and forced labor. The elders who had served Solomon gave Rehoboam the following recommendation: "If you will be a servant to this people today, and will serve them and grant them their petition, and speak good words to them, then they will be your servants forever" (v. 7). This was sound counsel and it would have been wise for Rehoboam to consider it.

Sadly, Rehoboam had another group of advisors—young men he'd grown up with and who now served on his court. They said he should increase the people's labor and taxes and assert his power over them so they would respect him.

Foolishly, Rehoboam forsook the recommendations of the elders and followed his young friends' advice. What followed was absolutely devastating for the nation. The people, unable to continue under the harsh conditions placed upon them, rebelled against Rehoboam and began following a man named Jeroboam son of Nebat—a leader who would prove self-serving, idolatrous, and wicked to the core. Jeroboam led the ten northern tribes of Israel to split off from the two southern tribes of Judah and Benjamin and become their own nation. That is why for centuries the northern tribes would be called Israel and the two southern tribes would be referred to as the nation of Judah.

But don't miss the point that Rehoboam and the nation of Israel paid a high price because he listened to the wrong advisors. Although our bad choices may not have such disastrous consequences as his did, we'd do well to learn from him by being very careful about who we allow to guide us. The goal in seeking wise counsel is to find someone who will tell us the truth based on what God says in His Word.

So how can you detect bad advice? Unwise counselors make either little or no mention of God or Scripture or they twist His message to suit their ideas. Their guidance will be based on what they think and what's acceptable in the culture, rather than what the Lord has taught is wise and true. In fact, unwise advisors may even show some defensiveness when you mention the Bible and often suggest a course of action that is far from biblical. For example, they may suggest a course by which you can escape your problems and pain—avoiding them by shirking responsibility or wronging another person. You know that is not what God desires. In fact, He may want you to walk through your difficulties with Him to increase your intimacy with Him, build your character, strengthen your faith, and free you from bondage.

Likewise, imprudent counselors may recommend reading material that is non-Christian and criticize the Christian leaders you listen to or godly people you know. In addition, you may notice an absence of prayer in your interactions with them. Remember, their goal will not be to help you find God's will or submit to Him in your decisions. Rather, they may wish to tell you what you want to hear in order to win your confidence and approval, to make you dependent on them, or even to control you. So be careful to avoid counselors with an ungodly lifestyle. This applies to both professionals and friends—non-believers and Christians. If someone is not living in submission to Christ, it's doubtful that he or she will be able to give godly advice.

Ignorance of God's Character and Principles

A third reason we may be hindered in hearing the Lord is because we don't really know God and His ways. Maybe you would say, "Well, as a believer, surely I know Him. I have received Jesus as my Savior. What more is there to understand about Him?" Oh, my friend, there is so much to learn about the Great I AM—the One Who has always been, Who will always be, and Who is to come. If you only know Jesus as your Redeemer, there may be a great deal you are missing about His will and how He operates. Even worse, you may not trust Him as deeply as you can because you don't truly know His character and how profoundly He cares for you.

Remember, knowing God's will means understanding how *He thinks* about your situation. This makes learning about Him and His principles absolutely crucial to your pursuit of making a wise decision. The less you know about Him, the less you'll know how to listen to Him, which in turn means the less you're going to hear from Him. But

> *God's will means understanding how He thinks about your situation.*

the more you understand about Christ and Who He is, the more you'll be able to perceive His activity in your circumstances.

For example, take the principle of brokenness. I spoke about it briefly when I talked about self-will and how God will work to liberate us from it. Brokenness is the Lord's method of dealing with our dependence on self and other things for our fulfillment and security. It is something that we are all guilty of at one point or another. In fact, you can see the Lord working out the process of brokenness in the lives of all the great biblical saints—Abraham, Joseph, Moses, David, Jeremiah, Simon Peter, Paul, and many others. The reason the process of brokenness is necessary is because no matter how committed we may be to God, we will always fight the inclination to do things our way rather than His. Thankfully, Christ has purposed to bring every area of our lives into submission to His will. So He continues to remove every obstacle until we surrender completely to Him and trust Him fully. He uses the difficulties we experience in order to transform us into His likeness—godly representatives who are equipped for all He has planned.

But you see, if a believer doesn't know about the principle of brokenness he or she might think that the unexpected times of hardship and waiting were a punishment. That in some way God was declaring through the trials that He had rejected the believer and was pouring out His wrath on him or her. However, that is an incorrect understanding of the believer's circumstances. Rather, the Lord permits times of difficulty in order to liberate us from false sources of security and to build us up for service.

That is why I encourage you to be in the Word of God daily. Because when you're in Scripture you're giving the Holy Spirit a fertile field in which to speak to your heart and teach you about Himself.

Sadly, many believers sitting in the pew today don't see why that would be important for them. They don't spend much time knowing God or growing their intimate relationship with Him. If they go to Him, it is with a list of requests rather than to know the One Who created them. They actually comprehend so little about the Lord that it's doubtful they could fill one side of a sheet of paper with facts they know to be true about Him. And even if they could, they couldn't tell you how those facts apply to their lives, circumstances, or relationship with Him.

But that doesn't have to be true for you. You can *know* God. You can become so intimately acquainted with Him that you can perceive how He is moving in your life. You may think, *Oh, that's just for pastors, preachers, prophets, and missionaries.* But no, it is not. This kind of intimate relationship is His will for you. James 4:8 says, "Draw near to God and He will draw near to you." The Lord answers whoever will seek Him and reveals Himself to those who long to know Him.

Unbelief

A fourth factor that can hinder you from hearing God's will is unbelief—a combination of fear in your heart about your situation and doubt concerning the Lord's promises or character. There are many believers who do not truly believe that God speaks today or that He is able to lead them. Certainly, they think Scripture provides them with moral guidelines for living. But they do not really have faith that the Father will speak to them personally or come through for them in the crucial moments of their lives.

So what I want to ask you is this: Are *you* fully convinced that Almighty God does indeed communicate with you about your life, family, work, finances, wounds, frustrations, and fears? Do you truly believe that He still speaks today, but more specifically, that He speaks to you personally and helps you with the issues you care about deeply?

We may all desire to respond, "Yes, absolutely!" to such questions. But it becomes more difficult when we consider the command of Proverbs 3:5–6: "Trust in the LORD with all your heart and do not lean on your own understanding. In all your ways acknowledge Him, and He will make your paths straight." It is very challenging to our faith when what God chooses to reveal does not make sense to us or frightens us in some way. But just because we do not comprehend or like the Lord's plan does not give us a right to doubt it.

Just because we do not comprehend or like the Lord's plan does not give us a right to doubt it.

Remember this during the times when you do not see your way clear. Because there *will be* moments in your walk with Jesus when He will only show you what you must do for your next step instead of disclosing the entire plan to you. You will feel like saying, "Lord, what are You doing? Why have You allowed all of this? How are You going to work all of this out?" These are the instances when you're in danger of doubt and fear taking hold. When you are susceptible to falling to unbelief and turning off His path for you.

I have seen this often in my life. I can look back at many times when God revealed only part of the plan. But if I had waited until I got the full picture, I would have missed His will. That is the way the Lord operates. He gives you sufficient light in order to travel to the next point on His road map. When you reach that place, He gives you the next clue on the journey. This is the way He works, because it teaches you to be fully dependent on Him.

If He showed us the full story and how to do everything at one time, we'd go prancing off in our own way, doing our own thing. Next thing you know, we're stepping off a cliff, because we think, *I've got this down*. We would immediately forget Him and take shortcuts that would eventually lead us to destruction. That's why the will of God usually comes a step at a time. He knows that we would bypass the very obstacles and challenges that prepare us and make the journey successful. But we simply cannot lose doing what God wants us to do, when He wants us to do it, and in the manner He says to proceed. This is the most certain way to success.

So one of the wisest things you can do when you wake up in the morning and before you go to bed at night is take time to be by yourself—quiet and alone—and just allow the Father to talk to you about your day and about what is coming up. Cultivate a listening ear and give God time to speak in His own way and in His own time. Because when you do—when you keep your relationship with Jesus strong and vibrant—you are less likely to fall to unbelief or to stray when the path is unclear.

Feelings of Unworthiness or Guilt

The fifth factor that can hinder you from hearing God is how you feel about yourself—if you see yourself as unworthy of His love and concern. You may not think this has anything to do with hearing the Lord, but it does. If you have a poor self-image and don't understand your identity in Christ, you may unintentionally wonder, *Why would God ever speak to me or care about the way I take? I'm not anybody. I'm not someone who merits His direction. Why should I think God's going to say anything to me?*

Now, this has to do with an internal sense of inferiority or inadequacy because of how you were raised or what others have communicated to you about your worth. But it can also be true if you constantly feel a sense of guilt for the things you have done wrong and the ways you have failed. This can be an issue whether you feel *true* guilt—remorse for actual sins—or *false* guilt for transgressions that have already been forgiven. Either way, you may feel as if you can never live up to the Lord's holy standard—as if you can never measure up or truly please the Father.

If you live in bondage to those destructive feelings—either unworthiness or guilt—it will be difficult to hear the Father because of your own negative thoughts toward yourself. You will do most of the talking and it's going to be self-centered—more about how you don't deserve Him than how wonderful He is or what He desires to do through you.

So what I would say to you is this: Listen to your thoughts. Think about what you think about. This may sound ridiculous to you, but it will show you what is truly dominating your communication with the Father. Because if you are continually saying, "God isn't going to speak to me," "I don't deserve His love," "I hate myself. How could He love me?" or, "Look what I've done—I just don't think He could forgive me," or any variation of those messages, then no matter how loudly He speaks to you, you won't believe it. And the truth of the matter is that you may almost be afraid to listen to God. You already feel so condemned that you don't want to hear how else you fall short of His holy standards.

But, friend, you must see yourself as God sees you—as His beloved, blood-bought child who needs His divine guidance and grace every day. Jesus has forgiven your sins and made you acceptable and worthwhile. He has sealed you with His Holy Spirit. Think of that: You are worthy of being the dwelling ground of His Spirit and of being His representative in this lost world! If that were not true, He would have taken you home to heaven immediately after you accepted Christ as Savior. But He didn't because you have a story to tell. You have had your sins forgiven. And there are others who need to hear how profoundly God has set you free.

See yourself as God sees you—as His blood-bought child who needs His divine guidance and grace every day.

So fight those feelings of inferiority and guilt with the truth of Scripture.

+ When you feel you are too insignificant for God to care about you, remember Isaiah 43:1–2: "Thus says the LORD, your Creator, O Jacob, and He who formed you, O Israel, 'Do not fear, for I have redeemed you; I have called you by name; you are Mine! When you pass through the waters, I will be with you.'"

✦ When the enemy bombards you with the lie that you are damaged without hope, recall what 1 Corinthians 5:17 says about you: "If anyone is in Christ, he is a new creature; the old things passed away; behold, new things have come."

✦ When you think, *What could the Lord possibly want with me? I'm worthless*, replace that thought with 1 John 3:1: "See how great a love the Father has bestowed on us, that we would be called children of God."

✦ When you're tempted to believe, *I know that the reason I am suffering is because God has rejected me*, fight that lie with the truth of Psalm 34:18: "The LORD is near to the brokenhearted and saves those who are crushed in spirit."

✦ When you've done something you think God could never forgive, claim the truth of 1 John 1:9: "If we confess our sins, He is faithful and righteous to forgive us our sins and to cleanse us from all unrighteousness."

✦ When you feel defeated and the thought crosses your mind, *I am a sinner to the core*, remember Romans 8:1: "There is now no condemnation for those who are in Christ Jesus."

✦ When you begin to believe that you cannot forgive yourself, meditate on Psalm 51:6–7: "You desire truth in the innermost being, and in the hidden part You will make me know wisdom. Purify me with hyssop, and I shall be clean; wash me, and I shall be whiter than snow."

+ When you are tempted to believe, *That mistake will always be with me*, count on what Psalm 103:12 says: "As far as the east is from the west, so far has He removed our transgressions from us."

+ When you feel like you are at rock bottom and no one could ever love you, remember what God has said in Jeremiah 33:3: "I have loved you with an everlasting love; therefore I have drawn you with lovingkindness."

+ And when you don't think God could possibly bless you with the deepest desires of your heart, remember Psalm 84:11: "The LORD God is a sun and shield; the LORD gives grace and glory; no good thing does He withhold from those who walk uprightly."

The God Who created the millions of different species of insects, plants, and animals, Who formed all the planets, constellations, and heavenly bodies and put them all in their orbits, the Sovereign King Who knows and rules everything, cares *for you*. And He has given His Son so that you can know Him. So stop second-guessing yourself and start praising the One Who makes you worthy. He has good things in store for you and desires for you to experience the fullness of His joy.

Busyness

The sixth hindrance you may experience is busyness. Of course, you may well have legitimate reasons for having a full schedule. You may have to work extraordinary hours to meet the needs of your family or care for a loved one. But often when people are trying to avoid God, they fill their lives with activities in order to shut out the Holy Spirit's promptings. They stay busy.

So understand that when I talk about busyness I'm not speaking about your responsibilities and what you genuinely must do. Rather, I am talking about the fact that we all make choices about what we should do with our time—and often we may show that the Lord is our last priority by how much time we spend with Him. This can happen to anyone. I have even known pastors who have stayed so busy "serving God" they couldn't tell you when their last quiet time was or when they last heard from Him. Certainly, they may have prayed for others or read the Bible seeking out a sermon, but that is not the same as having deep, intimate fellowship with the Lord. Sadly, these ministry leaders fill their lives with so much activity that they do not have time to seek Him. And if they do not have a moment to bow before Him and understand His will, then they really never know what He actually desires for them to do.

There are many people who do the same thing. They run around all day trying to get things done, attempting to achieve what they desire, hoping they will make a difference. Then they come home to their house or apartment and immediately turn on the television, computer, music—or what have you—and always have something playing so they can avoid the quietness.

But you see, it is only what is done in obedience to God that lasts and makes a truly enduring difference (1 John 2:17). So if you are not consulting the Father about what He wants you to do, then much of what you are running after may be for naught.

> *It is only what is done in obedience to God that lasts and makes a truly enduring difference.*

For example, most of us can relate to the story found in Luke 10:38–42. Jesus went to visit a family He loved—Lazarus, Mary, and Martha. They were His dear friends and when Jesus arrived at their house, Mary stopped everything she was doing so she could listen to and learn from Him. Martha, however, was distracted by all that was still to be done, so she kept working. She also felt slighted that Mary wasn't helping with the chores.

In a culture that valued hospitality as theirs did, Martha's reaction was understandable. She wanted her home to be as comfortable and welcoming to Jesus as possible out of honor and respect for Him. This was not sinful. It was the accepted and *expected* practice. But this just goes to show that expectations can drive us—whether we have them for ourselves or others impose them on us. But they may also be steering in the wrong direction.

Because when Martha complained about Mary, Jesus replied, "Martha, you are worried and bothered about so many things, but only one thing is necessary, for Mary has chosen the good part, which shall not be taken away from her" (Luke 10:41-42). Christ affirmed Mary's choice to be with Him and urged Martha to follow her sister's example. Both women expressed their love and care for Jesus through their actions, but Jesus was clear—Mary had chosen the *better* way.

From their story, we learn that God's expectations for us may be very different from the ones we have for ourselves. Yes, He wants us to serve Him. But His even greater desire for us is that we spend time with Him because He knows that our effective service flows from our moments of profound, intimate communion with Him. As I so often say, our intimacy with God—His first priority for our lives—determines the impact of our lives. So we should never let busyness rob us of our chance to know the Savior better, because our relationship with Him is what truly makes a difference that lasts.

So how do you overcome your busyness when there seems so much to do? Begin by asking God what is truly essential and ask Him to teach you how to choose His best. A person who has learned to walk in the Spirit has discovered the awesome practice of living out his relationship with God as he carries out his responsibilities. It's always best to have a time set apart for interacting with Him—even if it is only ten minutes in the morning. But the truth of the matter is that we are always walking with the Lord.

While I was in college, I worked in the bleachery division of the Dan River textile mill for extra money. It was sweltering hot in there—usually over a hundred degrees—so it took only about twenty minutes for me to be soaking wet with perspiration. I really didn't like being there. The temperature was miserable and all you could hear were the terrible sounds of machines everywhere. It was deafening. You couldn't talk to anyone or hear anything else that was going on. But after about a week, I learned to use that noise for my benefit—to allow it to drown out everything but God. So as I worked on the machine I was assigned to, I made it my goal to talk to the Lord and listen to Him.

Friend, it makes no difference what your circumstances are; you can train yourself to listen to God in any kind of situation. You and I always have the ability to think about Him, meditate on His Word, talk to Him, and listen to Him no matter what we are doing. That is why we have the presence of the Holy

> *You can train yourself to listen to God in any kind of situation.*

Spirit indwelling us and taking every step with us. That is also what 1 Thessalonians 5:17 means when it says, "Pray without ceasing." We must always be aware that God is present with us and available to us.

Because the truth is that Jesus should be involved in everything that you're doing and you should be seeking His perspective on everything you encounter. Don't allow the world to crowd Him out. Don't permit an endless onslaught of non-critical tasks to usurp time you should be spending with Him. Because there is something so wonderful about coming to the end of a day when you have been aware of Him moment by moment and step by step. Instead, decide to seek God's presence at every turn. That will make an awesome difference in your life because you will experience His energy, peace, and fulfillment at the end of even difficult days.

God-Directed Anger

Of course, maybe you just don't believe what I just said about the benefits of being in the Father's presence. Perhaps you think the opposite is true—that He is not worthy of your attention or trust. And it could be that the reason you either consciously or unintentionally avoid knowing God's will is because of the seventh hindrance: unhealed anger and resentment you have toward Him.

This is a much bigger issue in Christian circles than anyone likes to admit. How can anyone be angry at the God Who sacrificed so much for our salvation? But the evidence is there. I've had people say to me:

"My wife died and I can't figure out why the Lord took her."

"My son was in the prime of his life and he passed away so suddenly. I don't understand why Jesus allowed that to happen."

"These horrible things happened when I was a child. Where was God? How could He have permitted that to happen to me? Why didn't He protect me?"

Because the Lord allowed some profound trial or adversity in their lives, that bond of trust is broken and the deep roots of fear and bitterness exist in their lives. Consequently, God-directed anger becomes one of the greatest hindrances to knowing the Lord's will. Because think about it—

can you really hear what someone else is saying when you are bitter, resentful, and hostile toward him or her? Not really. The person with whom you are angry may even speak to you out of love and kindness, but if unforgiveness rules your heart, you'll find it difficult to believe what he or she says.

The same is true with God. When people are angry with Him, they may tell the Lord their needs. But more often than not, they will continually refer to the past and mention events that happened that—to their minds—justify their unbelief or disobedience toward Him. They will say:

"If You hadn't let these things occur, I could trust You."

Or, "Lord, if You're everything the preacher says—if You're sovereign and You've got everything under control—why did You let that happen?"

Or, "I want to have faith in You, but it is so difficult because You allowed me to be hurt so terribly. How can I possibly rely on You to defend me or provide for me now?"

So when they pray, they are not trying to know Him or learn His will. They are really blasting the Lord—telling Him all the reasons why they think He is cruel and cannot be trusted. Because the truth of the matter is that anger is rooted in fear. Somewhere deep within them they are waiting for the other shoe to drop—for God to do something or permit difficult circumstances that will wound them even further. And they want no part of that.

Friend, you can't hear anybody you're resentful toward. So search your heart: Are you angry at God? This is not something that is easy to admit, especially if you have been a believer for a long time. But if you find any resentment within you for terrible experiences the Lord did not prevent or important requests He did not grant, it is indeed possible that your bitterness is preventing you from knowing God's will. Likewise, if you are in constant fear of what will happen or the trials He has planned for you, then there is undeniably a problem with how you see Him.

The apostle John explains the inherent issue: "There is no fear in love; but perfect love casts out fear, because fear involves punishment, and the one who fears is not perfected in love" (1 John 4:18). In other words, if you fear God's mistreatment, then you do not really know how much He loves you and how much He has given for you. The Father cares for you deeply and unconditionally. He allows challenges in your life so He can teach you to walk more closely with Him, free you from bondage, and develop your character. They are never for your harm—not ever. Rather, when God touches something in your life and there is fear or anger there, it is because there is a deep wound that requires healing. He works in those painful areas for you to be fully free of whatever is destroying you.

> *"There is no fear in love; but perfect love casts out fear, because fear involves punishment, and the one who fears is not perfected in love."*
> *—1 John 4:18*

How do I know this? Because that is who God is. Psalm 86:13 says, "Your lovingkindness toward me is great, and You have delivered my soul from the depths of Sheol." The Living Bible paraphrases the same verse like this: "You love me so much! You are constantly so kind! You have rescued me from deepest hell." Yes, that means He frees you from eternal damnation. But it is more than that. Your Father wants you to be completely liberated from the enslavement to sin and the suffering it causes you. "If the Son makes you free, you will be free indeed" (John 8:36).

Think about it: Has the Lord ever hit you back when you've blasted Him? When you've expressed your anger, has He ever argued with you or poured His wrath out on you? Do you know why He doesn't? Because your Savior understands the deep and excruciating hurt you feel (Heb. 2:17–18). He realizes the wounds that your experiences have caused in you. He has compassion and mercy toward you and works for you to be healed of the pain that plagues you. Isaiah 30:18 (NIV) affirms: "The LORD longs to be gracious to you; therefore he will rise up to show you compassion. For the LORD is a God of justice. Blessed are all who wait for him!"

Your heavenly Father loves you. Yes, He cares for you even though you blame Him for the events of your past. Even though your view of Him is misinformed by your experiences. Even though as those terrible things happened to you, He was there faithfully protecting and sustaining you in ways you could not even conceive because of the love He has for you. He recognizes why you are angry and why you fear what could happen to you.

So I need to repeat what I told you in chapter 2, and that is: *Do not fear!* Often we may be afraid that God will allow us to be hurt deeply again. That is why we don't listen to Him and have trouble seeking Him.

I can remember in seminary, for example, every year there were big mission conferences that were very powerful. Missionaries would come from all over the world and talk about the awesome things the Lord was accomplishing in their ministries. It was very inspiring. But I recall speaking to a fellow who refused to go to the mission conference because he was afraid that God would call him to be a missionary.

Do you see that? He was fearful of what the Lord would ask him to do because he was sure it would be something he wouldn't like. Somewhere in his past, roots of bitterness and distrust were planted deep in his heart.

I asked him as kindly and compassionately as I could, "So you think that because you avoided the mission conference—and possibly hearing

God call—you've set yourself free from doing His will, whatever it might be?" I hoped he could see the error in his thinking—especially as a man called to serve God in ministry. But in truth, I felt sorry for him because he did not understand that ultimately what the Father was calling him to do was what he was created to accomplish—what he was *formed* for and would give him the greatest degree of satisfaction and joy. Instead, this fellow was taking the dangerous risk of disobeying God and living the rest of his life wondering what the Lord would have done if he had obeyed Him.

Friend, this is what harboring bitterness toward God does—it deafens you to the Father's call and good, acceptable, and perfect purposes. Don't make the same mistake. Let go of your resentment and anger toward God. Set your mind and heart on comprehending how profoundly He loves you and grow in your love for Him. Do not fear His will; instead, respect what God says and honor Him by obeying His leadership. Yes, He may call you to accomplish assignments that scare you. The issue isn't whether you fear or not; rather, it is whether or not you do as He says, trusting that He knows what is best for you. Because He absolutely does—and you don't want to miss it.

Willfully Harbored Sin

The eighth and final factor that can hinder you from hearing God's will is harboring sin. Now, we all sin and fight battles with temptation. That is part of our struggle between the flesh and the Spirit. However, there comes a point when we pass from committing a sin to harboring it—to embracing and shielding it as part of who we are and what we are entitled to. This happens as God addresses something in our lives and we ignore Him. He tells us, "Beloved, this is hurting you. It no longer fits who you are as my child. I want to set you free and truly meet that need in your life, but you have to let go of this destructive habit." You know exactly what that is because it immediately comes to mind. But you've become enslaved to it—you refuse to let it go.

That harbored sin is clouding your vision, dividing your mind, and distracting from the abundant life your Father desires for you. It is like putting cotton in your ears—dulling your sense of hearing to what God has to say to you.

> *Willfully harboring sin is like intentionally putting cotton in your ears—dulling your sense of hearing to what God has to say to you.*

Sin is one of the greatest hindrances to hearing the voice of God. You won't hear Him clearly when sin is clouding your mind, your will, and your emotions.

For example, in the previous chapter I spoke of Samson, who was a prophet of the Lord during the time of Israel's judges. From his conception, Samson was called to the Nazirite vow (Num. 6), which was a pledge of separation and dedication to the Lord.

This Nazirite vow meant Samson:

+ *Could not drink wine or consume any product made from grapes.* He could not even touch them.

+ *Could not eat any unclean thing.* He was to obey the usual dietary laws of the Israelites.

+ *Could not have his hair cut.* This was a peculiar instruction considering that Paul wrote: "If a man has long hair, it is a dishonor to him" (1 Cor. 11:14). So Samson was required to release his desire to be accepted by the Israelite society and be seen as a respected man.

✦ *Could not touch a dead body.* Because the dead were considered unclean, Samson would not be able to be around the deceased, including family members who had passed away.

These requirements may seem to be quite restrictive, and they are. However, Samson was consecrated—or set apart—in this manner to show he belonged to the Lord and his life was a platform for His power.

The problem is that Samson was focused almost entirely on his own desires rather than God's will. Before he ever got to Delilah, Samson had violated most of his Nazirite vow. In Judges 14:8–9, he touches the carcass of a lion and eats honey out of it. Of course, the honey would have been made unclean just by its location in the lion, and touching a dead body was in direct violation of his Nazirite vow. He further violates this aspect of his consecration when he uses the "fresh jawbone of a donkey"—a newly deceased animal—to kill a thousand Philistines (Judg. 15:15).

Likewise, Samson is often reported as being in the Philistine Valley of Sorek, where the city of Timnah was located, an area famous for its vineyards. Judges 14:10 tells us, "Samson made a feast there, for the young men customarily did this." These types of celebrations normally involved a great deal of drinking. Remember, Samson's call was to avoid grapes and grape products altogether. His consistent presence in a land and at events known for wine is counter to what his consecration called for.

Therefore, by the time Samson gives in to Delilah and tells her the secret of his hair he has almost completely violated his Nazirite vow. In fact, the cutting of his hair was the last strand of the pledge left undefiled. So in that moment, when Samson told Delilah his secret, what he was really doing was making Delilah his god. More specifically, Samson was choosing the appetites he was trying to fill through her—love, companionship, and sexual intimacy—over the Lord.

The cutting of his hair was not actually what removed Samson's strength. Rather, Judges 16:20 tells us: "The LORD had departed from him." Samson's life no longer had power because the Lord was no longer present with him. Of course, we know this is because God no longer ruled the throne of Samson's heart.

We may think, *How could Samson have been so stupid?* But this happens to us whenever we choose to harbor sin rather than trust God to provide for us. Samson was merely trying to fulfill his needs in his own way—just as sometimes we might try to do. And as we know, that led to the Philistines blinding him and putting him in prison.

In a similar manner, the Father may allow us to continue on in our sinful habits for a while. But eventually, as with Samson, He shows us that what we are doing is not working for us and is actually destructive to us.

So what could Samson have done to avoid such a tragic ending? First, he could have taken God seriously. The Lord had formed Samson to lead Israel out of bondage to the Philistines—this powerful call was known even before Samson was born (Judg. 13:3–5). But because he was so focused on his own desires, he missed God's will.

Likewise, Samson could have stopped and asked, "What will this decision cost me?" at each crossroad on his path. Many times, when we take a moment to think seriously about what we are doing we realize that the consequences are not worth the risk. So when you are tempted by sin, ask yourself, "What will my actions do to my relationship with Jesus?" While the Lord has promised to love you, He also expects you to love Him in return, obeying His commands.

Finally, Samson could have and should have noticed that he no longer heard from God. Judges 16:20 tells us this sad truth: "He did not know that the LORD had departed from him." Samson was so far from God that he never even noticed when His Spirit left him. What a tragedy!

However, this is instructive to us. Because sometimes we are living our lives, engaging in sins the Lord cautioned us to avoid, and we don't even really notice that we haven't heard Him speak in a while. But then some trial or issue arises in our lives and we desperately need to hear from the Lord. We want His counsel and guidance. We long for His provision and grace.

I have seen this repeatedly in my ministry. I've sat down with people and they've told me the challenges they faced and how desperate they felt.

I always ask, "Have you asked the Lord about this?"

"Yes, I've asked Him about it."

"What did He say?"

"He didn't say anything."

"Nothing?"

"I'm praying and asking God to show me what to do, but He hasn't said a thing. He is silent."

Throughout my life, I have learned an important principle about God's silences: ***Most of the time, when the Father is quiet it is because there is something within you He has already pointed out and He wants you to deal with it.*** Notice, I said "most of the time." This does not always apply. But usually, when someone is having trouble hearing the Lord at all it is because there is something He has already told that person to do and he or she has ignored Him—sweeping the issue under the rug and refusing to deal with it.

> *Most of the time, when the Father is quiet it is because there is something within you He has already pointed out and He wants you to deal with it.*

If this is the case with you, understand it is important to Him that you address it because it is crucial to your spiritual health that you overcome it. You are only hurting yourself by refusing to give up your addiction, sinful actions, or destructive coping mechanisms.

When I have experienced such times and dealt with the attitudes or behaviors in question, God's will became crystal clear to me. The same will be true for you.

Therefore, the wisest thing you can do is pray, "Deal with me, God. Show me what it is in my life that is blinding me to Your will. And give me the strength and wisdom to turn away from the sinful attitudes and behaviors that are preventing me from following You in obedience. In Jesus' name, amen."

Whatever the Lord reveals to you, agree with Him that it is a problem. Confess your sin and do as He says to turn away from it. And trust your loving heavenly Father to fill your deepest needs in a more profound and wonderful way than you have ever imagined.

Sharpening How You Hear

The greatest treasure apart from knowing the Lord Jesus Christ as your personal Savior and having His Spirit indwell you is understanding God's purpose and plan for your life. Don't miss out on that awesome gift because of your self-will, the influence of others, ignorance of God's character and principles, unbelief, feelings of unworthiness or guilt, busyness, God-directed anger, or willfully harbored sin. It is just not worth it.

Instead, pray through the following list of questions and ask God to evaluate you. Do not ignore anything He tells you. Write it down and realize it is an area He wants to work on to sharpen how you are able to hear Him.

+ What do I spend most of my time thinking about? What do I see as the greatest objective of my life or the most important desire of my heart? Is there a driving goal in my life that is more important to me than God? Am I trying to get my way despite what He may be calling me to?

+ Am I experiencing brokenness in any area of my life? What is the Lord communicating to me through the trials and challenges I am facing?

+ Are the people speaking into my life godly? Is there anyone who consistently tries to control me or move me away from God's will? Am I allowing that person undue influence in my life? How is he or she affecting how I make decisions? How does that relationship need to change? Is there anyone the Lord is directing me to seek as a wise and godly counselor?

+ How well do I know God? Is my lack of understanding about His character and what pleases Him hindering me from hearing Him? Am I operating on any unsubstantiated beliefs about who He is or how He operates? Do I have a grasp about how He thinks about my life?

+ Am I fully convinced that Almighty God wants to communicate with me about my life, family, work, finances, wounds, frustrations, and fears? Do I truly believe that He still speaks today, but more specifically, that He speaks to me personally and helps me with the issues I care about deeply?

✦ Am I leaning on my own understanding of the challenges before me? Am I doubting God because I just don't comprehend what He is doing or do not see His hand in my circumstances? Can I trust Him to lead me one step at a time?

✦ Is there anything I perceive about myself that I believe prevents me from having an intimate relationship with Jesus? Is it my sense of identity? Are there negative messages from my past that I need to counteract with the truth of Scripture?

✦ Do I live with a sense of guilt over something I have done? Have I ever asked God to forgive me for it? If not, why not? If so, do I not believe He is able to truly pardon me? That is not coming from Jesus, Who forgives all my sins past, present, and future; so what is it in me that believes I am unforgivable? Do I really believe that I am that powerful that I can commit a sin Jesus cannot forgive?

✦ Have I been too busy to take time for God? Is it because I am genuinely doing crucial, needed work or am I avoiding Him? Am I filling up my life with activity in an attempt to fill my own needs of acceptance, worth, and capability? Is my activity drowning Him out? What can I cut out of my life to make more time for Jesus? How can I make sure He is involved in everything I am doing?

✦ Am I angry with God? When I speak to Him do I praise Him or give Him reasons I don't trust Him? Is there something in my past that I blame Him for? Is there some unfulfilled request that has planted a root of bitterness in my heart? Am I waiting for the other shoe to drop—for the next bad thing to happen?

+ Do I really believe God loves me? Do I really believe He will never leave or forsake me? That He has my best interests at heart and works everything out for my good? If not, what caused these mistaken beliefs? What does Scripture say about the issues I struggle with?

+ Am I avoiding knowing God's will? Why? Am I afraid of God's will? If so, what is the real reason?

+ Am I repeatedly committing the same sin in my life? What need do I think this sin is filling? Is it actually satisfying my deep need, or is it really making me feel worse about myself and creating more problems? Why don't I trust God for this need? Do I really believe He cares about the profound needs I have?

+ Has God been silent toward me? What was the last thing He told me to do? Why do I find it so difficult to obey His command? Am I afraid of losing something?

+ What can I do today to take a step of faith in obedience to Jesus?

As I said, pray through these questions and don't ignore anything the Father reveals to you. Instead, write it all down and ask Him for His wisdom. If you need to pray through the list a few times—every day for a week or a month—do so. And obey everything the Lord says. You will be amazed at how God cleans out your heart and helps you to hear Him.

The Father will not always speak to you in the way you expect—but He will speak to you. And once you truly hear His voice and experience what it's like to walk in His will, you won't want to live any other way. So don't fight Him. Seek Him, submit to Him, and watch Him make more of your life than you ever imagined possible.

6

CAN I BE SURE?

Committing to God's Glorious Plans for Your Life

Can you know the will of God for your life? After you read this book I hope you both know and are confident that you can. You can know His will in the grand, overarching plan He has for you and in the decisions you must make every day. You can learn to hear Him at the great crossroads and in the smallest details. That is the truth of the kind of relationship the Lord your God wants to have with you.

However, there is one more thing I wish to discuss with you before we end this journey together. Because the truth of the matter is that at times the Lord will call you to do things that appear unreasonable to your human viewpoint. Likewise, there will be seasons when you have been pursuing God's will—you know you heard Him and are obeying Him, but you have no evidence of His activity in your circumstances. Then there will be moments that you are doing exactly as the Lord commanded, but everything seems to go disastrously wrong.

We only have to look at King David and know that these three situations are often true in the lives of people walking in the center of God's will:

1. ***Doing the unreasonable.*** We know that God called David to fight Goliath, a Philistine warrior many times his size and weight and with much more military experience and preparation (1 Sam. 17). Although Goliath was fully clad in armor and was equipped with both a javelin and spear, David had only the clothes on his back, a slingshot, and some stones. There was no part of this that was a fair fight. Even worse, the future of Israel was at stake. How could a boy like David ever hope to overcome a professional giant-warrior like Goliath? To human eyes, this was a no-win scenario. But God.

2. ***Waiting with no evidence of deliverance.*** David had been anointed as the next king and promised the throne of Israel (1 Sam. 16:13). However, there came a point when the sitting king, Saul, became so jealous of David that he commanded his servants to kill him (1 Sam. 19:1). David spent years on the run—many of them outside the land of Israel. One might imagine the many nights that David slept on the ground in a foreign land—far from Israel or the kingly life he was promised—that he would grow discouraged with his circumstances. Where was the Lord Who had called David? Had He forgotten David or the anointing He had placed on him? How could He allow David to reach such a point of utter removal from the promise? It seemed absolutely, totally impossible that David would ever become king of Israel. But God.

3. ***Disastrous setbacks.*** Then there was the time when David settled in Ziklag—a city of Gath (1 Sam. 30). Sadly, while David and his men were away, the Amalekites raided Ziklag, burned

their encampment, and captured their wives and children. David's men were so devastated that they sought to kill him. So in the midst of his heartbreak over his family, David had to deal with the pain of betrayal and the fear of losing his life. How could David rule the *nation* of Israel if he couldn't even lead and protect the small, insignificant *city* of Ziklag? If even his small army of men wanted to kill him, how could he ever engender the love and trust of the Israelite people? It seemed ridiculous to think the Lord had really chosen him. But God.

You can see these scenarios played out over and over again throughout Scripture and in the lives of all the biblical saints. I have faced such circumstances in my own life repeatedly. So it is not a stretch to think that you may well encounter such faith-stretching times as well. This is because God wants you to make the decision to trust Him even when all evidence seems contrary to His stated promises and path. Will you rely on your senses or Him? Will you lean on your own understanding or trust in the Lord with all your heart (Prov. 3:5–6)?

> *God wants you to make the decision to trust Him even when all evidence seems contrary to His stated promises and path.*

However, it is in such instances that you need assurance. How can you be sure that you heard the Father correctly and that what you are experiencing is all part of His ultimate plan? How can you, like David and the other saints of Scripture, know God is still in the midst of your situation and guiding your footfalls?

Because these are the times it is most important that you express *faith*. You don't want to step out of God's will when the going gets tough, because the consequences of doing so are too great. And often the pressure to give up is most extreme right before the Lord provides the most important breakthroughs concerning the promises He's made. You don't want to miss His best for you. So it is crucial for you to be absolutely certain of His will.

Sevenfold Test to Confirm God's Will

With this in mind, here is a sevenfold test that will help you determine whether or not a particular decision or plan is God's will for your life. I pray that you will write these down on a three-by-five card, like I asked you to do for the eight points about how to discover God's will in chapter 4. Jot these questions down and keep them next to that other card. And as you seek the Lord's plan for your life and sense He is moving you in a certain direction, ask these questions. Confirm His will. And be listening for the promptings of the Holy Spirit, because He will guide you in taking the right path.

Is it consistent with the Word of God?

The first and most important point, of course, is whether or not what you sense God is telling you to do is consistent with the whole counsel of Scripture. This is because, as I often say, the Father would never tell you to do anything that contradicts His Word. So you can always be confident in looking to the Bible for direction.

However, I wish to give you a caution at this point. Often, when I've taught this principle, people think that finding a verse of Scripture or two that *justifies* what they desire to do is sufficient. But that is not what I mean. Yes, it is wonderful to have promise verses that you can claim. That is crucial, and whenever God gives you a promise verse it is wise to write it down and commit it to memory.

But what is even more important is that we always take into account the *whole counsel* of Scripture—that we form our decisions based on principles that are found throughout God's Word, rather than an isolated, out-of-context verse or two. We can see a great example of this in the life of David. As I said earlier, Saul became so jealous of David that he wanted to have him killed. In fact, 1 Samuel 23:14 (TLB) reports: "Saul hunted him day after day, but the Lord didn't let him find him." So David was forced to flee the land and the people he loved.

> *Always take into account the* whole counsel *of Scripture.*

You can imagine David's surprise, however, when he was given not one but two opportunities to kill Saul (1 Sam. 24, 26). Now, if we were to put ourselves in David's shoes, our human rationale might go something like this:

1. God has promised me the kingdom through the prophet Samuel.

2. God has given me this opportunity to kill Saul—not once, but twice.

3. The prophet Samuel told Saul, "The LORD has torn the kingdom of Israel from you today and has given it to your neighbor, who is better than you" (1 Sam. 15:28). So taking Israel from Saul is the Lord's will.

4. Saul has done some terrible things that have dishonored God and harmed Israel—including viciously killing the priests and

people of Nob (1 Sam. 22:6–19) and consulting the witch of Endor (1 Sam. 28:5–20).

5. If I do not kill Saul, my men may rebel against me.

6. If I do not kill Saul, he may succeed in killing me.

7. I have been faithful to God and have waited a long time for this through some very difficult circumstances. Perhaps this is His reward to me—to kill the man who has caused me so much pain.

That would seem like an airtight case for David to take Saul's life. However, David did not. Instead, to *both* opportunities he said, "Far be it from me because of the LORD that I should do this thing to my lord, the LORD's anointed, to stretch out my hand against him, since he is the LORD's anointed" (1 Sam. 24:6). In other words, God had put Saul on the throne and only the Lord could take him off the throne. That was not a privilege that David enjoyed. And David understood this because he knew God's Word.

As I discussed in chapter 3, you can know for certain that it is never part of God's desired plan for you to lie, steal from others, commit murder, or have an adulterous affair, because the Lord states that clearly in His Word (Exod. 20:13–16). Yes, David was a man of war who killed enemies such as Goliath. However, he did so in defense of Israel when there was no other choice but to fight and be God's vessel in the battle. Recall what David told Goliath: "You come to me with a sword, a spear, and a javelin, but I come to you in the name of the LORD of hosts, the God of the armies of Israel, whom you have taunted. This day the LORD will deliver you up into my hands, and I will strike you down . . . that all the earth may know that there is a God in Israel . . . for the battle is the LORD's and He will give you into our hands" (1 Sam. 17:45–47).

But to kill Saul—a man whom God had chosen (1 Sam. 9:16–17)—would provide no such testimony to the world. Instead, it would betray David's lack of faith that the Lord "removes kings and establishes kings" (Dan. 2:21).

We must remember this always because it is so easy for the enemy to take and twist Scripture to suit his purposes. Remember, Satan quoted God's Word when tempting Jesus during those forty days in the wilderness. And how did Jesus fight him? With God's Word (Matt. 4:5–7).

What Satan did reveals the problem that arises when we proof-text a passage or take it out of context to justify our stance or actions. For example, you cannot say you are being compassionate by stealing from one person and giving to someone else. Biblical principles remain consistent throughout the whole counsel of Scripture—you cannot violate one command to fulfill another. Likewise, you know that "the fruit of the Spirit is love, joy, peace, patience, kindness, goodness, faithfulness, gentleness, self-control; against such things there is no law" (Gal. 5:22–23). The Lord's plan can and should produce this fruit in you. If a situation makes you hateful, bitter, vengeful, restless, self-centered, greedy, untrustworthy, harsh, and reckless, it is probably not God's will. Rather, it is when you act out of your God-given love, joy, peace, et cetera—when these traits pour forth from you supernaturally—that you know you are acting in a godly manner and in accordance with the Lord's plan.

Now, I realize that you may be worried that you don't know enough of the Bible to decide whether or not something is God's will. But remember, His Word is a lamp to your feet and a light to your path (Ps. 119:105). Your Father will give you sufficient illumination right where you are. However, you will continually need more light as the path goes on.

Therefore, one of the principles we can glean is that God's plan will *always* drive you *to* His Word for guidance, courage, strength, confirmation, and wisdom. If something you are considering causes you to avoid Scripture for any reason, you can know for certain it is not His will. But if you are in a time of testing and your goal and desire is to draw near to God—you are hungry for His Word and compelled to seek His presence—then know you are on the right path.

> God's plan will always drive you to His Word for guidance, courage, strength, confirmation, and wisdom.

Is this a wise decision?

The second question you should ask about any course of action is: *Is this a wise decision?* How will this choice you are making shape your future? Are there consequences because of it that aren't in God's plan for your life? Because sometimes it is the unwise choices we make while we are walking in His will that cause us difficulty.

The example that immediately comes to my mind is that of the Thessalonian believers who had heard that Christ's return was imminent. Some of them were so convinced Jesus would appear immediately that they quit their jobs and felt it was unnecessary to work any longer. However, nowhere had the Savior ever said to do such a thing. They may have believed they were expressing faith in His return by doing so. Others may simply have thought that it was acceptable to take advantage of the kindness of other believers until He came. But their actions actually showed an incredible lack of wisdom. After all, Jesus Himself said, "Of that day and hour no one knows, not even the angels of heaven, nor the Son, but the Father alone" (Matt. 24:26). There was absolutely no assurance anywhere that He would return before their supplies ran out.

The idea that "an idle man will suffer hunger" (Prov. 19:15) is not a concept that is only found in Scripture, either. Seven centuries before Jesus, the Greek poet Hesiod declared, "Idleness is a disgrace." Two hundred years before Christ, the Roman playwright Plautus wrote: "He that would eat the nut must crack the shell." Two decades before Jesus walked the earth, the Roman poet Horace penned: "Life gives nothing to a man without labor." So the concept that laziness is unwise is one they would have recognized regardless if they'd read Scripture or not. Even the unbeliever understood the necessity of work.

But as Christians, they did have the testimony of God's Word to guide them.

+ Proverbs 6:9–11: "How long will you lie down, O sluggard? . . . Your poverty will come in like a vagabond and your need like an armed man."

+ Proverbs 12:24: "The hand of the diligent will rule, but the slack hand will be put to forced labor."

+ Proverbs 13:4: "The soul of the sluggard craves and gets nothing, but the soul of the diligent is made fat."

+ Proverbs 20:4: "The sluggard does not plow after the autumn, so he begs during the harvest and has nothing."

Likewise, Christ often spoke of the wise stewardship of resources—of investing what a believer has in the kingdom of God and being a blessing to others (Matt. 25:14–28; see also Eph. 4:28).

So when Paul wisely admonished them, "If anyone is not willing to work, then he is not to eat, either" (2 Thess. 3:10), it should not have come as a surprise to them.

Paul was clear: They were sinning against God when they failed to provide for their own needs and refused to do what Christ had called them to do, which was preach the gospel. These lazy believers were not only using up valuable resources that should have been used for spreading the good news of salvation and ministering to others but also preventing other believers from serving effectively because they demanded so much attention.

So there are principles of wisdom that can and should guide your decisions. You can learn many of them if your will read the book of Proverbs. But always remember: "The fear of the LORD is the beginning of wisdom, and the knowledge of the Holy One is understanding" (Prov. 9:10). Make your decisions with God in mind. Honor Jesus with your actions. Remember that there are people watching to see how you are living so they can make a decision about Him. And always consider that if you pursue your treasure or your pleasure here on earth, it will pass away (Matt. 6:19–20). But if you spend your life investing in Christ's eternal kingdom, it will produce "fruit that will last" (John 15:16 NIV). For "the world is passing away, and also its lusts; but the one who does the will of God lives forever" (1 John 2:17).

Can I honestly ask God to enable me to achieve this goal?

The third question that would be good to ask is: *Can I honestly ask God to enable me to achieve this goal or to support this course of action?* Does what you are seeking fit who He is? Is it appropriate for you to ask for it as someone who represents Him in the world? We must ask these questions because in the midst of walking in God's will we can be waylaid by seeking out blessings that do not match His character.

Of course, there are people who say you can request absolutely anything from our gracious heavenly Father. Although I agree that He is kind and generous, I do not believe that everything we ask for is appropriate. For example, you cannot ask the Lord to bless sin—He just won't do it. It is an affront to His character for you to ask Him to approve of your dishonesty, allow you to gain from thievery, or satisfy ungodly lusts.

Obviously, we all know that. However, sometimes I believe that we still ask Him for things that are clearly stated in His Word because we believe ourselves to be the exception to His rules.

For example, I cannot tell you how many times young Christians have come to me saying they believe it to be God's will that they marry an unbeliever and ask me to pray the Lord will allow them to wed. Their significant others don't come with them to church, read the Word of God, or show any interest in being saved. "But," they will tell me, "I'm so in love and happy about our relationship. It is absolutely wonderful."

Privately I am thinking, *Sure, temporarily.*

You see, there is a reason God has commanded, "Do not be bound together with unbelievers" (2 Cor. 6:14). Marriage is difficult enough without having two different kingdoms—the kingdom of God and the rule of the world—working against each other in it. Paul explains, "What partnership have righteousness and lawlessness, or what fellowship has light with darkness? Or what harmony has Christ with Belial, or what has a believer in common with an unbeliever? Or what agreement has the temple of God with idols?" (vv. 14–16). He names what is diametrically opposed because that is what happens when a Christian marries a non-Christian. There are two different spirits ruling the believer and the non-believer—and whether we want to admit it or not, they are continually at war with each other.

Oh, things may appear fine before the vows are spoken. And the believer may think that somehow he or she can win his or her loved one to Christ. However, repeatedly I have seen that it comes at a terribly great cost. If the person does accept Jesus—and only one in a multitude does—it has only ever been after a very long and painful struggle. As I have said, I have seen this end in disaster too many times to count.

But the point is: Is this a course of action that we can legitimately ask God to bless? After all, God gave marriage as a beautiful picture of His relationship with us (Rom. 7:1–4; Eph. 5:25–32). And He has commanded in His Word that we not be unequally yoked with unbelievers. Understanding these two principles should guide anyone who is considering marrying an unbeliever in making a wise decision.

Likewise, throughout my life I've seen plenty of people who wanted the Father to bless schemes that would not bring honor to the name of Jesus but rather shame. For example, I recall knowing a believer who wanted to steal the technology of a competing company in order to further his interests. In fact, he asked me to pray about it, claiming that his ownership of such information could eventually assist missionaries in their efforts. He was trying to dress up an ungodly scheme with a seemingly noble goal. But such deceptive tactics never turn out well and do excessive damage, bringing reproach on Christ and those who believe in Him. Galatians 6:7–8 is clear: "Do not be deceived, God is not mocked; for whatever a man sows, this he will also reap. For the one who sows to his own flesh will from the flesh reap corruption, but the one who sows to the Spirit will from the Spirit reap eternal life."

> *"The one who sows to the Spirit will from the Spirit reap eternal life."*
> —Galatians 6:8

Remember, if you are walking in the will of God the enemy is going to use whatever he can to get you off the path. He knows your greatest temptations and weaknesses. So the Lord is not going to cater to destructive, fleshly desires—no matter what they may be or why you may have them. He is not going to condone anything in your life that prevents you from being conformed to the image of Jesus or from Christ to be exalted in a godly manner (Rom. 8:29). And if you do happen to manipulate your circumstances to the point that you acquire something outside of God's will, the likelihood is that it will turn to ashes.

Don't do it, friend. Don't waste your time on what won't last. Do not fall to the tactics of the enemy. If you're tempted to ask the Lord for something that you know is contrary to His character, realize it's not His will for you and you must not pursue it.

Do I have genuine peace about this path?

A fourth question that is wise to ask is: *Do I have genuine peace about this path?* I spoke about contentment being a component in the discovery of God's will in chapter 4. So it is only logical that our sense of tranquility should persist as we travel in the center of His path for our lives.

Of course, you may be wondering, *Is it really possible to walk through the storms of life and be at peace when everything around seems to be working against me?* After all, we are talking about when you are in need of confirming God's will in the midst of unreasonable circumstances and challenges, long delays without any view of deliverance, and disastrous setbacks. When you feel beleaguered, your world is crashing around you, and you cannot see the road ahead, can you really, genuinely feel God's peace?

Yes, my friend, you can.

That is why it is peace "which surpasses all comprehension" (Phil. 4:7). It does not make sense. But remember how this tranquility occurs: "In everything by prayer and supplication with thanksgiving let your requests be made known to God. And the peace of God, which surpasses all comprehension, will guard your hearts and your minds in Christ Jesus." You go before the Lord God in prayer—seeking His guidance and provision. You give Him thanks, remembering who He is and all He has done for you. And as you do, He gives you the assurance that He is with you. He also either confirms that you are on the path of His will or corrects your course.

We know this because in Greek the word *peace, eirene,* means, "to bind together." Essentially, when you have the peace of God it is because you are joined with Him—in unity and agreement with His purposes and course for your life. It is a sense of calmness that cannot be explained, but you know it when you have it. You kneel before the throne of grace and every bit of your anxiety melts away. Yes, your dreams may seem to be falling apart, but you have this deep, internal sense of confidence that somehow you will make it through and see the great promises God has given you fulfilled.

When you have the peace of God it is because you are joined with Him—in unity and agreement with His purposes and course for your life.

This is what David spoke of when he said, "I would have despaired unless I had believed that I would see the goodness of the LORD in the land of the living. Wait for the LORD; be strong and let your heart take courage; yes, wait for the LORD" (Ps. 27:13–14). In other words, every reason for desperation and desolation is in view. Hope at this point makes no earthly sense at all. But rising up from deep within me is this absolute, total certainty that I will see God do what He has said. So I will take courage and wait for Him. It might not yet be His time to bring this promise to fruition, but I know He will come through when the time is right.

Have you ever felt this deep assurance? The proof of it comes in your time alone in your Savior's presence. Do you experience peace when you kneel before Him? If your choices are causing you to feel restlessness when you pray or you're motivated to avoid Him altogether, you can be certain that the path you're asking about is not in line with His plans for you. But if you are overwhelmed with His love, power, and peace though everything is crashing around you, you know you are right where you're supposed to be.

Is this decision appropriate for who I am as a follower of Christ?

The fifth question to ask is: *Is this decision appropriate for who I am as a follower of Christ?* In other words, would you recommend the choices you're making to another Christian? If other believers knew about your conduct would they approve? If a lost person knew what you were doing would he or she be drawn *to* Jesus or *away* from Him?

Because one of the important things that happens when you walk in God's will is that He will root out the attitudes and habits that no longer fit your new identity in Christ. Remember His goal, which I discussed in chapter 2. His objective in your life is to conform you to the likeness of Jesus (Rom. 8:29). He is molding you to bear:

+ **Jesus' character**—to think as your Savior does and behave in a manner that exalts Him, so others may believe and be saved.

+ **Jesus' freedom**—releasing you from the bondage of sin so you can walk in His complete liberty.

+ **Jesus' confidence**—His unwavering faith and assurance in the Father and His promises.

+ **Jesus' obedience**—His perfect submission to God's will.

+ **Jesus' heart**—with self-sacrificing grace and compassion toward others and passion for God's holiness.

+ **Jesus' focus**—which was always fully set on the Father, accomplishing His plans, in His ways and timing.

+ **Jesus' mission**—to help others know and experience God in an eternal, unbroken relationship and become His fully devoted followers.

+ **Jesus' power**—that the very power of the resurrection may be demonstrated in and through your life so that others might know the Living God.

That is the Lord's goal for you. However, as you are walking on the path of His will there are behaviors that you inherently know are not appropriate for you as His redeemed child. It may be the way you gossip, walk away from commitments, engage in some addictive behavior such as ingesting illicit substances or committing sexual sins, spend excessive time and focus on secular activities, or harbor unforgiveness in your heart. It may not directly be related to or the cause of the trial you are experiencing, but God keeps bringing it to your attention as something that must be purged from your life.

You know what it is because you most likely hide those actions from others. You may even feel some embarrassment whenever you engage in them and you know that they would tarnish your testimony if anyone knew what you were doing. But the Father keeps bringing it up whenever you are alone with Him. And don't be fooled; it is not only the big offences that He targets. *Anything* that harms your body, mind, or spirit is not the will of God—and He *will* go after it. In fact, it may well seem like what He is revealing to you should not matter, that what you do seems so minor to you that He couldn't possibly be interested in it. But

> Anything *that harms your body, mind, or spirit is not the will of God— and He* will *go after it.*

He is because in some manner it is affecting your life and preventing you from becoming more like Jesus. And no amount of praying or Bible reading will make up for it. You must root it out.

Friend, shame and humiliation are never God's will for you. If there are activities in your life that harm you or cause you to feel dishonor, confess them to your heavenly Father, repent of them, and allow Him to lead you into the glorious freedom He desires for you as His child. Make the choice, give up the attitude or habit, and be like Jesus. Because that is the way you can be sure to become all He created you to be.

Does this fit God's overall plan for my life?

The sixth point of examination is whether or not what you are doing fits God's overall plan for your life. As I have said repeatedly throughout this book, the Lord has great purposes for you. When you are in the midst of trials or trying to confirm His will, it may not seem that way because it is still a matter of faith. However, the Lord is very interested in making sure that you do not chase a side goal that would ultimately harm His purposes for you.

For example, several years ago a friend of mine offered to build me a house on a beautiful island. He had some land there he wanted to donate and said he would love it if I would accept it as a gift. He gave me the name of an architect and told me that I could design it however I wanted it—that he would be glad to construct it for me out of gratitude for the way God had used me in his life. It sounded like a dream come true.

Naturally, I thought, *Wow, Lord, You're really blessing me! You are so good!*

I began making some plans with the architect and sketching out what I wanted in this dream house.

But as I prayed about it, I knew God was saying, "Don't take that."

Of course, I asked, "Why, Lord?" Why would God prevent me from taking such a fantastic gift? It was a chance in a lifetime to own an extraordinary piece of property for free. I could not understand how it could negatively affect my life. In fact, I had already begun planning how I would go there for a spiritual retreat—to pray and spend time in His presence as I made important decisions.

Likewise, what would my friend say? I didn't want to offend him. It was such a kindhearted and lavish gesture.

I could think of a million reasons to take the gift. But there was one reason not to—and that one overrode them all. The Lord had said, "No."

So I went to my friend and explained that I could not accept his generous offer; that God would not allow me to take it. My friend wanted to know why, and I could not tell him. I was so embarrassed, and I know he felt slighted by my refusal.

Some time later, the Lord opened my eyes to how He had protected me from a disastrous mistake. Unbeknownst to me, this man had made it a practice to ingratiate himself to pastors—buying them extraordinary gifts. Then, when they were indebted to him, he would compel them to push his agenda. He would tell them what to preach and what topics to avoid. Accepting that house would have absolutely ruined my ministry.

Thank God for His wisdom! Because of His guidance, I am free to preach however He directs. He never, ever leads us wrong.

Understand that the Father is at work in a similar way in your life. Through the difficult decisions, disappointments, obstacles in the road, and challenges, He is preventing you from getting involved in what distracts you from His overall plan or could derail you altogether. Yes, the disillusionments and setbacks hurt. Yes, at times it will feel like the sacrifices are too great to handle. But know this for certain—the Father has designed you with His excellent reasons in mind and He will protect the wonderful goals He desires to accomplish through you. Remember that Psalm 139:13–16 declares:

> You formed my inward parts; You wove me in my mother's womb.
> I will give thanks to You, for I am fearfully and wonderfully made;
> wonderful are Your works, and my soul knows it very well. My
> frame was not hidden from You, when I was made in secret, and
> skillfully wrought in the depths of the earth; Your eyes have seen
> my unformed substance; and in Your book were all written the days
> that were ordained for me, when as yet there was not one of them.

From before you were even conceived, the Lord took great pains to design your features and make a plan for your life, your potential, and all you could accomplish. He formed you with great care. You are singular. Important. A valuable part of His church. There has never been nor will there ever be another person like you. He loves you unconditionally, sincerely, and uniquely—as if you were the only person on earth. And your part in His plan is crucial. You have no idea whose eternity may change because of your faithful obedience to God.

In light of this then, it is always important for you to consider whether your choices support or oppose His path for your life. Because if you choose to deny His direction and stray from His plan, you will ultimately be forfeiting what you were created for. And that, my friend, is something that would be truly terrible indeed.

Will this decision honor God?

The seventh and final question it is wise to ask is: *Will this decision honor God?* Because, if you think about it, glorifying the Lord and living in respectful reverence to Him should be the ultimate goal of our lives.

This is why the *Westminster Shorter Catechism* of 1674 teaches: "Man's chief end is to glorify God, and to enjoy Him for ever." We exist because it gave the Lord joy to create us, and our response to His goodness and love should be to exalt Him.

> *This is what knowing and doing the will of God is all about—revealing Him to others by exalting Him in our lives.*

Revelation 4:11 tells us: "Worthy are You, our Lord and our God, to receive glory and honor and power; for You created all things, and because of Your will they existed, and were created." This is what knowing and doing the will of God is all about—revealing Him to others by exalting Him in our lives.

Certainly, we all do so in the unique way the Father has given us to do so.

But now think of this in terms of the trials you are experiencing and what they tell you about His will. It may not seem very glorifying to the Lord that you would face unreasonable obstacles, long delays, or difficult setbacks. Yet is it?

+ Because it is in ***attempting the unreasonable*** when our strength and resources are not sufficient that the Lord's power shines through. Think about David's fight with Goliath that I spoke of at the beginning of this chapter. As I said, there was no part of that battle that was fair—David was so outclassed by his giant Philistine opponent that no one would ever have expected him to win. But as 1 Corinthians 1:27 says, "God has chosen the weak things of the world to shame the things which are strong," David *could not win*—he simply did not have the strength, training, or equipment to do so. Yet this showed that the victory had to come from a source outside of himself. In this manner, the Lord showed that it was *His* victory that day. And that is also true in the overwhelming obstacles and challenges you face. You cannot handle it, so God can show that He is the One Who does.

+ Likewise, ***David spent a long time waiting with no evidence of deliverance.*** We know that between the time he was anointed to be the king of Israel and when he actually took the throne was approximately two decades. How does such a delay glorify God?

But remember, the Lord says, "I am God, and there is no one like Me, declaring the end from the beginning, and from ancient times things which have not been done, saying, 'My purpose will be established, and I will accomplish all My good pleasure' . . . Truly I have spoken; truly I will bring it to pass. I have planned it, surely I will do it" (Isa. 46:9–11). There is no glory in predicting the predictable. In other words, God allows circumstances to appear absolutely contrary to what He has promised to show that what stands forever is His Word—not what we perceive with our senses to be true. He declares, "So will My word be which goes forth from My mouth; it will not return to Me empty, without accomplishing what I desire, and without succeeding in the matter for which I sent it" (Isa. 55:11).

And so the Lord shows that in the long delays and our impossible circumstances what we see and experience cannot override what He has planned. David became king of all Israel, just as God promised. The Lord will fulfill His promises to you as well. Truly, He always "acts in behalf of the one who waits for Him" (Isa. 64:4).

✦ Finally, God's glory can be seen in **_disastrous setbacks._** As I discussed, David faced a devastating defeat at Ziklag, when the Amalekites raided the city, burned their encampment, and captured their wives and children, and his men turned on him. If there was ever a time that a soul wanted to lie down and die because of all that had happened to him, I would imagine this could have been that moment for David. Instead, however, 1 Samuel 30:6 reports: "David strengthened himself in the LORD his God." David got back up. He got back on his feet. He sought the Lord and was able to track down the Amalekites, retrieve his loved ones and everything that was taken, and restore his good standing with his men. Verse 19 reports: "Nothing of theirs was missing, whether small or great, sons or daughters, spoil or anything that they had taken for themselves; David brought it all back."

But as we saw in chapter 2, this is the difference between the believer and the lost person; those who have faith and those who don't; those who have a true relationship with God and are walking in His will and those who are merely going through the motions—the ability to get up and keep going. As Proverbs 24:16, instructs, "The godly may trip seven times, but they will get up again" (NLT).

It is through that kind of perseverance that these great and terrible pressures glorify God—they show how His supernatural power sustains us during the most difficult trials we experience. The apostle Paul explains it like this: "We do not want you to be unaware, brethren, of our affliction which came to us in Asia, that we were burdened excessively, beyond our strength, so that we despaired even of life; indeed, we had the sentence of death within ourselves so that we would not trust in ourselves, but in God who raises the dead" (2 Cor. 1:8–9). In other words, we do not have it in us to survive the burdens and hardships we endure, so it can only be the Savior's resurrection power that allows us to keep going.

This becomes our testimony and ministry to those around us. Or as Paul explains in 2 Corinthians 1:3–4, "The God and Father of our Lord Jesus Christ . . . comforts us in all our affliction so that we will be able to comfort those who are in any affliction with the comfort with which we ourselves are comforted by God." We not only become able to persevere through His resurrection strength, but we also help others to endure as well.

So consider, in the midst of your circumstances, are you demonstrating your respect and reverence for the Father? Is it evident by your actions that He is the Lord of your life? Or are you really relying on and serving something or someone else?

As I discussed in the previous chapter, the Lord will not tolerate anything coming before Him in your priorities. So if you find yourself exalting anyone or anything other than God in what you're experiencing, then you have taken a turn off the path of His will. However, if even during the worst difficulties you wish to honor Him, if Your goal is to exalt Him through your pain, if you keep going because you know your God is able to help you despite everything that's happened, then know that you are still on track. Keep seeking Him. Keep trusting Him. And keep getting back up. Because in that way you will show that "the surpassing greatness of the power" that flows in and through your life is from God and not from you (2 Cor. 4:7). And that will certainly glorify Him.

Commit to His Will

So as you seek assurance of God's will, consider these questions carefully and prayerfully:

+ Is it consistent with the Word of God?

+ Is this a wise decision?

+ Can I honestly ask God to enable me to achieve this goal or to support this course of action?

+ Do I have genuine peace about this path?

+ Is this decision appropriate for who I am as a follower of Christ?

+ Does this fit God's overall plan for my life?

+ Will this decision honor God?

When you can say yes to these seven questions, you know you have confirmed God's will. However, do not get frustrated if you cannot answer these questions immediately. Sometimes you may run a decision or a course of action through those questions several times before you know His will for sure. But in time, the Father will make it crystal clear if you are on the right path or if your course needs adjustment. As I have said throughout this book, you can absolutely always trust Him to speak to you.

Likewise, I realize that you may be seeking the answer to a decision that God has not revealed to you yet. Even as you've read through this book the course may have become a little clearer, but you may not be entirely certain what His direction is. This is because although the Lord cares about the choice that is weighing on your mind, His greater goal is to deepen your relationship with Him. So He doesn't just want to answer a question in your heart; rather, He wants to form a pattern for you to relate to Him in every aspect of your life. He desires for you to be continuously aware of His goal for you, the ways He speaks to you, what may be hindering His will, and how you can confirm His path for you.

So commit to doing God's will—not only in the present decisions before you, but for your whole life. Refer often to the components of discovering His will:

+ Communion with God Through Scripture

+ Circumstances of Life

+ Counsel of Godly Christians

+ Conscience

+ Common Sense

+ Compulsion

+ Contentment

+ Communication with God Through Prayer

Make them a daily part of your life. Periodically, examine whether there are any hindrances thwarting your relationship with Him: self-will, the ungodly influence of others, ignorance of God's character and principles, unbelief, feelings of unworthiness or guilt, busyness, God-directed anger, or willfully harbored sin. Review the seven questions for confirming His will as often as you need, realizing that you have Almighty God on your side to show you exactly what He wants you to do.

Finally, always be willing to do whatever your heavenly Father says—no matter how big or small, practical or unreasonable, easy or difficult, popular or unpopular, rewarding or costly. Always say yes to Him.

Always say yes to Jesus.

Even when you don't want to, even when you are afraid, even when you don't understand His direction, even when it is painful—remember that Jesus is the One Who saves you, forgives your sins, sanctifies you, provides for you, protects you, gives you a home in heaven with Him, and loves you unconditionally and eternally.

So say yes out of love and gratitude to Jesus.

Say yes because you know He would never steer you wrong.

Say yes because the Lord your God is worthy of your obedience.

Say yes because He "causes all things to work together for good to those who love God, to those who are called according to His purpose" (Rom. 8:28).

Say yes because all things are possible with Him and "no good thing does He withhold from those who walk uprightly" (Ps. 84:11).

Say yes because He knows what He has created you for—"plans for welfare and not for calamity to give you a future and a hope" (Jer. 29:11).

Say yes because your Savior has the very best purposes for your life.

Say yes because His path is always right.

Because when you do the will of God, you cannot lose.

So let your Savior give you the abundant blessings and the fullness of joy He has planned for you. Say yes to God's will. Because when you do so, you will experience life at its very best and rewards in eternity beyond imagination.

Father, how grateful I am for the person who is holding this book and seeking Your will. You have formed Your child with Your great wisdom and purposes in mind. I pray for Your child and this awesome adventure of Your will that You have planned for his or her life. Thank You that it is a good, acceptable, and perfect plan. Thank You that it is a plan that will ultimately conform him or her to Your image—to Your character, freedom, confidence, obedience, heart, focus, mission, and power. I ask that You would draw Your child closer than he or she has ever been and that he or she would delight in walking with You and obeying You daily. Lord God, clear out anything that is hindering Your child from knowing You intimately. If there is something impeding his or her relationship with You, I ask that You would convict Your child of it in a manner that would leave no doubt in his or her mind and would compel him or her to repent. Help Your child to hear You clearly and see Your awesome face.

Lord God, I do not know the burdens and challenges of the person holding this book. What I do know is the great love You have for him or her and that Your plan is life at its very best. If Your child is facing overwhelming obstacles and challenges, sustain him or her with Your mighty strength, provision, and power. If Your child is facing long delays, give him or her patience and fill him or her with assurance of Your promises. And if Your child has had disastrous setbacks, heartbreaking losses, and devastating failures, remind him or her that You are near to the brokenhearted and save those who are crushed in spirit (Ps. 34:18). Give Your child confidence of Your presence and help him or her glorify You in all difficulties. And continuously remind Your child of Your great love for him or her, while filling his or her heart with love for You.

Help Your child to know and do Your will, O God. No matter how difficult or costly Your commands, give him or her the wisdom, courage, strength, love, and desire to follow You in obedience. Empower Your child to serve You and others with love, joy, peace, patience, kindness, goodness, faithfulness, gentleness, and self-control (Gal. 5:22–23). Because I know the plans You have for him or her are awesome. And I know that there is nothing more worth pursuing in this world than Your face and Your purposes.

Thank You for hearing my prayer for Your child. To You be all the honor, glory, power, and praise forever, Lord Jesus. In Your name I pray. Amen.

Appendix

PROMISE VERSES ABOUT GOD'S WILL

+ "Seek the LORD your God, and you will find *Him* if you search for Him with all your heart and all your soul. When you are in distress and all these things have come upon you, in the latter days you will return to the LORD your God and listen to His voice. For the LORD your God is a compassionate God; He will not fail you."

—Deuteronomy 4:29–31

+ "Be strong and courageous, do not be afraid or tremble at them, for the LORD your God is the one who goes with you. He will not fail you or forsake you. . . . The LORD is the one who goes ahead of you; He will be with you. He will not fail you or forsake you. Do not fear or be dismayed."

—Deuteronomy 31:6, 8

+ "Be strong and very courageous; be careful to do according to all the law which Moses My servant commanded you; do not turn from it to the right or to the left, so that you may have success wherever you go. This book of the law shall not depart from your mouth, but you shall meditate on it day and night, so that you may be careful to do according to all that is written in it; for then you will make your way prosperous, and then you will have success. Have I not commanded you? Be strong and courageous! Do not tremble or be dismayed, for the LORD your God is with you wherever you go."

—Joshua 1:7–9

✦ "Oh give thanks to the LORD, call upon His name; make known His deeds among the peoples. Sing to Him, sing praises to Him; speak of all His wonders. Glory in His holy name; let the heart of those who seek the LORD be glad. Seek the LORD and His strength; seek His face continually. Remember His wonderful deeds which He has done, His marvels and the judgments from His mouth."

—1 Chronicles 16:8–12

✦ "You will make known to me the path of life; in Your presence is fullness of joy; in Your right hand there are pleasures forever."

—Psalm 16:11

✦ "Who is the man who fears the Lord? He will instruct him in the way he should choose."

—Psalm 25:12

✦ "I will instruct you and teach you in the way which you should go; I will counsel you with My eye upon you."

—Psalm 32:8

✦ "The young lions do lack and suffer hunger; but they who seek the LORD shall not be in want of any good thing."

—Psalm 34:10

✦ "I will cry to God Most High, to God who accomplishes all things for me."

—Psalm 57:2

✦ "The LORD God is a sun and shield; the LORD gives grace and glory; no good thing does He withhold from those who walk uprightly."

—Psalm 84:11

✦ "The LORD will work out his plans for my life—for your faithful love, O LORD, endures forever."

—Psalm 138:8 (NLT)

✦ "You formed my inward parts; You wove me in my mother's womb. I will give thanks to You, for I am fearfully and wonderfully made; wonderful are Your works, and my soul knows it very well. My frame was not hidden from You, when I was made in secret, and skillfully wrought in the depths of the earth; Your eyes have seen my unformed substance; and in Your book were all written the days that were ordained for me, when as yet there was not one of them."

—Psalm 139:13–16

✦ "Teach me to do Your will, for You are my God; let Your good Spirit lead me on level ground."

—Psalm 143:10

✦ "Trust in the LORD with all your heart and do not lean on your own understanding. In all your ways acknowledge Him, and He will make your paths straight."

—Proverbs 3:5–6

✦ "The godly may trip seven times, but they will get up again."

—Proverbs 24:16 (NLT)

✦ "Those who seek the LORD understand all things."

—Proverbs 28:5

✦ "The LORD of hosts has sworn saying, 'Surely, just as I have intended so it has happened, and just as I have planned so it will stand.'"

—Isaiah 14:24

✦ "The Lord longs to be gracious to you, and therefore He waits on high to have compassion on you. For the Lord is a God of justice; how blessed are all those who long for Him. O people in Zion, inhabitant in Jerusalem, you will weep no longer. He will surely be gracious to you at the sound of your cry; when He hears it, He will answer you. Although the Lord has given you bread of privation and water of oppression, He, your Teacher will no longer hide Himself, but your eyes will behold your Teacher. Your ears will hear a word behind you, 'This is the way, walk in it,' whenever you turn to the right or to the left."

—Isaiah 30:18–21

✦ "Do not fear, for I am with you; do not anxiously look about you, for I am your God. I will strengthen you, surely I will help you, surely I will uphold you with My righteous right hand."

—Isaiah 41:10

✦ "Thus says God the Lord, who created the heavens and stretched them out, who spread out the earth and its offspring, who gives breath to the people on it and spirit to those who walk in it, 'I am the Lord, I have called You in righteousness, I will also hold You by the hand and watch over You."

—Isaiah 42:5–6

✦ "I am God, and there is no other; I am God, and there is no one like Me, declaring the end from the beginning, and from ancient times things which have not been done, saying, 'My purpose will be established, and I will accomplish all My good pleasure' . . . Truly I have spoken; truly I will bring it to pass. I have planned it, surely I will do it."

—Isaiah 46:9–11

✦ "So will My word be which goes forth from My mouth; it will not return to Me empty, without accomplishing what I desire, and without succeeding in the matter for which I sent it."

—Isaiah 55:11

✦ "From days of old they have not heard or perceived by ear, nor has the eye seen a God besides You, Who acts in behalf of the one who waits for Him."

—Isaiah 64:4

✦ "'I know the plans that I have for you,' declares the LORD, 'plans for welfare and not for calamity to give you a future and a hope. Then you will call upon Me and come and pray to Me, and I will listen to you. You will seek Me and find Me when you search for Me with all your heart.'"

—Jeremiah 29:11–13

✦ "Call to Me and I will answer you, and I will tell you great and mighty things, which you do not know."

—Jeremiah 33:3

✦ "Then the LORD answered me and said, 'Record the vision and inscribe it on tablets, that the one who reads it may run. For the vision is yet for the appointed time; it hastens toward the goal and it will not fail. Though it tarries, wait for it; for it will certainly come, it will not delay.'"

—Habakkuk 2:2–3

✦ "Ask, and it will be given to you; seek, and you will find; knock, and it will be opened to you. For everyone who asks receives, and he who seeks finds, and to him who knocks it will be opened."

—Matthew 7:7–8

✦ "Whoever wishes to save his life will lose it, but whoever loses his life for My sake and the gospel's will save it."

—Mark 8:35

✦ "This is eternal life, that they may know You, the only true God, and Jesus Christ whom You have sent."

—John 17:3

✦ "We know that God causes all things to work together for good to those who love God, to those who are called according to His purpose."

—Romans 8:28

✦ "Those whom He foreknew, He also predestined to become conformed to the image of His Son."

—Romans 8:29

✦ "Therefore I urge you, brethren, by the mercies of God, to present your bodies a living and holy sacrifice, acceptable to God, which is your spiritual service of worship. And do not be conformed to this world, but be transformed by the renewing of your mind, so that you may prove what the will of God is, that which is good and acceptable and perfect."

—Romans 12:1–2

✦ "Whatever was written in earlier times was written for our instruction, so that through perseverance and the encouragement of the Scriptures we might have hope."

—Romans 15:4

✦ "It is written, 'Things which eye has not seen and ear has not heard, and which have not entered the heart of man, all that God has prepared for those who love Him.' For to us God revealed them through the Spirit; for the Spirit searches all things, even the depths of God. . . . Now we have received, not the spirit of the world, but the Spirit who is from God, so that we may know the things freely given to us by God. . . . He who is spiritual appraises all things, yet he himself is appraised by no one. For who has known the mind of the Lord, that he will instruct Him? But we have the mind of Christ."

—1 Corinthians 2:9–10, 12, 15–16

✦ "We are His workmanship, created in Christ Jesus for good works, which God prepared beforehand so that we would walk in them."

—Ephesians 2:10

✦ "It is God who is at work in you, both to will and to work for His good pleasure."

—Philippians 2:13

✦ "Forgetting what lies behind and reaching forward to what lies ahead, I press on toward the goal for the prize of the upward call of God in Christ Jesus."

—Philippians 3:13–14

✦ "We have not ceased to pray for you and to ask that you may be filled with the knowledge of His will in all spiritual wisdom and understanding."

—Colossians 1:9

✦ "We urge you, brethren, admonish the unruly, encourage the fainthearted, help the weak, be patient with everyone. See that no one repays another with evil for evil, but always seek after that which is good for one another and for all people. Rejoice always; pray without ceasing; in everything give thanks; for this is God's will for you in Christ Jesus. Do not quench the Spirit; do not despise prophetic utterances. But examine everything carefully; hold fast to that which is good; abstain from every form of evil. Now may the God of peace Himself sanctify you entirely; and may your spirit and soul and body be preserved complete, without blame at the coming of our Lord Jesus Christ. Faithful is He who calls you, and He also will bring it to pass."

—1 Thessalonians 5:14–24

✦ "Jesus our Lord, equip you in every good thing to do His will, working in us that which is pleasing in His sight."

—Hebrews 13:20–22

✦ "If any of you lacks wisdom, let him ask of God, who gives to all generously and without reproach, and it will be given to him."

—James 1:5

✦ "You are a chosen race, a royal priesthood, a holy nation, a people for God's own possession, so that you may proclaim the excellencies of Him who has called you out of darkness into His marvelous light."

—1 Peter 2:9

✦ "The world is passing away, and also its lusts; but the one who does the will of God lives forever."

—1 John 2:17